Curly Grandma's Letters

Anita Bryce

Curly Grandma's Letters
Writing to Kids & Capturing Your Autobiography

Tate Publishing & Enterprises

Curly Grandma's Letters
Copyright © 2008 by Anita Bryce. All rights reserved.

No part of this publication may be reproduced, stored in a retrieval system or transmitted in any way by any means, electronic, mechanical, photocopy, recording or otherwise without the prior permission of the author except as provided by USA copyright law.

Scripture quotations marked "NAS" are taken from the New American Standard Bible ®, Copyright © 1960, 1962, 1963, 1968, 1971, 1972, 1973, 1975, 1977, 1995 by The Lockman Foundation. Used by permission. All rights reserved.

The opinions expressed by the author are not necessarily those of Tate Publishing, LLC.

Published by Tate Publishing & Enterprises, LLC
127 E. Trade Center Terrace | Mustang, Oklahoma 73064 USA
1.888.361.9473 | www.tatepublishing.com

Tate Publishing is committed to excellence in the publishing industry. The company reflects the philosophy established by the founders, based on Psalm 68:11,
"The Lord gave the word and great was the company of those who published it."

Book design copyright © 2008 by Tate Publishing, LLC. All rights reserved.
Cover and Interior design by Joey Garrett

Published in the United States of America

ISBN: 978-1-60604-612-8
1. Family/Activities
2. Family/Grandparenting
09.03.12

Dedication

This book is dedicated to my mother, Vera Lou Lewis.
As mother to eleven children,
No words can genuinely convey her love.
No verse can sing the praise of her dedication.
No sorrow was deeper than ours on the day we lost her.

"Her children rise up and praise her;
Her husband, too, extols her" (Proverbs 31:28).

Acknowledgements

Thank you, my darling grandchildren; Megan Leigh Salzlein, Hannah Marie Salzlein, Riley Michael Travis, Bryce Matthew Travis, Emily Grace Salzlein, Maggie Caroline Salzlein, and Olivia Paige Travis for politely indulging an old lady's sagas and graciously assuming my letters were significant. Without you there would be no book.

Thank you to my brilliant and wonderful daughters, Mary Anjanette (Angie) Travis and Shannan Leigh Salzlein. You have made this little book possible by blindly and lovingly supporting my correspondence obsession. Thank you for saving and rescuing my letters for seven years.

A special thanks goes to John and Sarah Tiftickjian. This book would not have been possible without your professional advice and assistance, and most of all, your faith in this project.

Carmel Eich. Thank you so much for walking me through midnight computer lessons on the phone. You are a great tech support.

Thank you, Baba, for being Baba.

Many thanks go to Gartner Studios, Inc., Stillwater, Minnesota for allowing me to publish letters printed on the following stationery designs: Snow Family, Snowflake, Jolly Snowman, Santa, Green Daisy Gingham, Yellow Daisy, Daisy Border, and Bugs. Reprinted by permission.

Hello Kitty-Sanrio, Shelbyville, Tennessee. Reprinted by permission; Thank you Hello Kitty-Sanrio for allowing me to print a letter written on your Hello Kitty Stationery.

Property of Highlights for Children, Inc., Columbus, Ohio. Reprinted by permission; Thank you Highlights for letting me print letters decorated with your shiny stickers.

Thank you, Kathy Welliver of Lewis Elementary School, Ft. Meade, Florida; I am grateful to you for allowing me to print one of Megan's letters naming you as her teacher.

Becky Taylor, Postmaster of Vernon, Florida; Thanks to your help with Chapter 8, our letters will be delivered without delay.

Contents

Preface		11
Chapter 1	**Two Types of Letters:**	**13**
	Friendly	14
	Autobiographical	17
Chapter 2	**The Cycle of Correspondence**	**32**
	The Notebook	33
Chapter 3	**The Heart of Correspondence**	**36**
	Rule #1: Write	37
	Rule #2: Illustrate	45
	Facial Expressions	48
	Body Movements	49
	Rule #3: Make it Free	56
Chapter 4	**The Four E's**	**57**
	Easy	58
	Entertaining	62
	Engaging	71
	Everlasting	77
Chapter 5	**Hodgepodge and Mishmash**	**79**

Chapter 6	**Target Your Audience**	**89**
	Read Aloud Letters	89
	Babies and Toddlers	90
	Four and Five Years Old	103
	Transitional Audience	111
	Letter to the Independant Reader	120
	Six to Eight Years Old	120
	Eight to Eleven Years Old	131
	Twelve Years and Older	133
Chapter 7	**Protocol to Ponder**	**139**
Chapter 8	**The Envelope: Or How to Get Along with Your Postmaster**	**149**
	OCR?	150
	Delivery Address	150
	Return Address	151
	P.S.	153
Chapter 9	**An Inkslinger's Cupboard**	**154**
Chapter 10	**The Benefits of Correspondence**	**158**
Addendum		**165**
Resources		**166**
Quotations		**168**

Preface

Family is one of our greatest treasures. We cling to family for love, hope, support, and just about every other emotion. We pay a price for closeness, but we receive tenfold what we put into family. Parental love is deep and powerful, and it comes with rewards beyond our merit. After parenthood comes "grandparenting," for those of us who are lucky. Being a grandparent releases us from the tumultuous struggle of rearing the children we love to indulge and enjoy a new generation of children we love.

Regardless of how we connect with our grandchildren, we grandparents yearn to share with them our traditions and customs. We love telling stories about our childhood, and our grandchildren love hearing them. We fancy the idea of being the wise and generous elders, and yet we love the idea of playfully connecting with our grandchildren. Our grandchildren see us as chieftains, as sages, or as oracles benevolently illuminating knowledge and cheerfully dispensing wisdom. Yes, as grandparents we bask in the simple pleasure of devotion and the reciprocate wonder of our grandchildren's affection. For this reason, because of this very unique relationship, we owe it to our grandchildren to share and recount the traditions, customs, and legends of their birthright. We have a purpose, if not a responsibility, to pass on our life story.

United in our desire to share our past, we also bear the general uncertainty of how to do it in a meaningful way. Why not leave our past in letters? It's as simple as that. We can share stories about our family, schools, jobs, accomplishments, goals, children, and our whole life. Our memories are entertaining and informative to our grandchildren, and scribing them can be enjoyable and even therapeutic for us. The goal of this book is to help you write and compile your letters into a notebook that becomes your autobiography. What all of us would like is someone who will write our biography, but since that is not practical we will write our own autobiography—one letter at a time. The time has come to let your personal correspondence set a course for everlasting testimony and enduring legacy!

Corresponding regularly consumes much time and energy, but it is worth it! This book helps you approach letter writing through a defined method that fashions your legacy in a pleasurable and comprehensive manner. It explains how to share your history in an age-appropriate style, set up grandchildren for return correspondence, save the communication in a dossier, and reap the bonus of gaining a pen-pal in your grandchildren.

Letters to and from Curly Grandma are scattered throughout this book as examples of strategies and techniques. They are presented in original form with no corrections in grammar, spelling, punctuation, or usage. My hope is that these flawed letters will put readers at ease and encourage grandparents to begin corresponding, even if they feel insecure about their writing or language skills. Perfection is nice, but certainly not necessary for correspondence.

In case you are wondering about the silly Curly Grandma name, it is a gift from my first grandchild, Megan. As a toddler, she was confused about having two grannies. One Christmas, her mommy tried to help by explaining that one of her presents was from her granny with the curly hair (hair as big as Dolly Parton's). When I walked in the door, Megan met me with, "Curly Grandma!" No efforts to change the name were successful. The child was determined that I was, indeed, Curly Grandma. The years passed, and more grandchildren came along. Curly Grandma turned out to be a difficult name for toddlers to pronounce. As a result, I have been Turdy Drama, Crr Grr, Telly Dama, and DumDum. But, all the grandchildren eventually found their way to the correct pronunciation. As for me, I wouldn't trade my name for anything.

> Unprovided with original learning,
> unformed in the habits of thinking,
> unskilled in the arts of composition,
> I resolved to write a book.
>
> Edward Gibbon (1737–1794)
> English historian of Rome

Chapter 1

Two Types of Letters: Friendly and Autobiographical

Correspondence with your grandchildren can be approached in different ways. You can write friendly letters or autobiographical letters. Your letters can be staggered, sometimes friendly, sometimes autobiographical, or you can mix the styles within a single letter. It is easy to begin a letter with friendly writing, and then evolve into autobiographical information. Each topic in the following chart will be explained in this chapter and in following chapters.

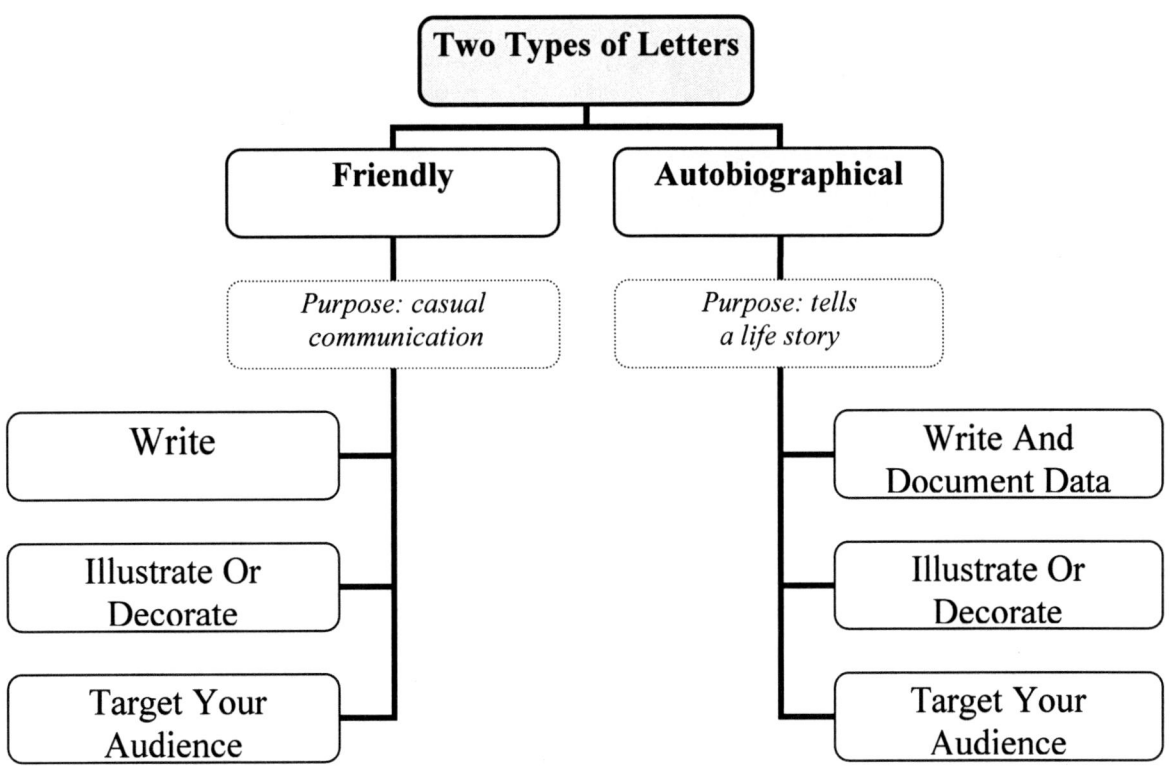

The purpose of a friendly letter is simply to communicate casually, while the purpose of an autobiographical letter is to relate a story from your past. Friendly letters are easy to write because they are often spontaneous and uncomplicated. Autobiographical letters must contain historical data. Both types of letters should be illustrated or decorated (see *Chapter 3: The Heart of Correspondence*), and both types should target the reader's ability to decode and comprehend (read and understand). Targeting the reader's ability is explained in *Chapter 6: Target Your Audience*.

Friendly Letters

Most of our letters are typical friendly letters. We learned about this kind of writing in elementary school. The following example of a friendly letter is to my oldest grandchild, Megan Leigh. Not yet eight years old, she was a good reader, and had just moved to the rural area near Fort Meade, Florida. I had just moved to the Gainesville area.

Letter to seven-and-a-half-year-old Megan

11-24-01

T I M B E R

Dearest Beloved,

I have been thinking about you quite a bit lately. I don't get much of a chance to write because I am so busy trying to design and build a house. You know how much time it takes Mommy to remodel her house, well I am doing nearly the same thing, so you see, I have my head into my computer and on the drawing table nearly all the time. I feel as though I go to sleep imagining how the house will look, and then I wake up thinking how the house will look. I never quit. But my relentless planning will pay off, I hope.

I will attach a floor plan (that is a plan of how the rooms will be arranged, some people call it a blueprint). So now, you will be able to see how much I have accomplished so far. If you have any ideas on how to improve my plan, please go ahead and mark on this plan and you can mail it to me or you can show it to me the next time I get to see you, which could possibly be this weekend, but I just don't know yet.

You will never imagine what I did today! We went out and cut down THREE trees! But, my Beloved, do not think these were just any trees. Oh no! These trees were very big and very old pine trees. These trees were 60 feet tall! These trees were 24 inches wide! These trees were as tall as 6 houses stacked on top of each other! I was so nervous because I thought they would fall the wrong way. When they did fall, I ran away as fast as I could. I was afraid they would fall right onto me. But they did not. They fell right where we wanted them to fall. My heart was pounding so fast and so hard, I thought my heart went right up into my throat. Believe me, this Curly Grandma doesn't get so much excitement in her life. So this experience today was one to write about!

Well, my Beloved, I do wish I could write some more, but I haven't the time because I must go study some books to figure out how many kitchen cabinets I must buy. I hope one day you can come to Gainesville and see my land, and then when the house is finished you can even see that!

So my love, take care of yourself, be safe, and be happy!
I ♡ u! I ♡ u! I ♡ u!
Thinking of you always,

Curly Grandma
Curly Grandma

It's as tall as 12 of me standing on top of each other

Here it comes! Get out of THE WAY!

Then this way →

It will land here

Run this way ←

WHEW!!

Pieces are falling!

Megan wrote back, and in her envelope she included the original floor plan that I sent to her. She made some changes: She drew a couch and a chair in the living room and a bed in the master bedroom.

Friendly letters are a real treat for children because they are relaxed and tailored to the child's reading ability. And, for the grandparent, it provides the opportunity to enclose little treasures such as:

stationery	stickers	stamps	notepads	puzzles
jokes	pictures	photos	books	magazines
pencils	candy	tiny toys	games	CDs

Newspaper funnies and magazine articles (age appropriate) are also great treats to include in a letter. All of these things can be obtained inexpensively, and most can be placed in an ordinary envelope. Some require padded envelopes. The tiniest treasures have weight and that adds cost, so be careful.

Just for fun, you can write letters on shapes. For example, your Valentine letter could be written on heart-shaped paper or a Christmas letter could be written on a snowman shape.

If you live in a place that is geographically different from the child's; for example how beach living contrasts with a mountain home, it is fun to include objects such as flowers, tree leaves, or bird feathers from your area. (It is against the law to mail feathers of migratory, threatened, or endangered birds, so check with local authorities on which flora and fauna are off limits.) Explain how they are different from those where the child lives. You could begin a "What is it?" correspondence. Send a piece of something unique to your area, let the child figure out what it is, then in the next letter or package send the whole thing or the answer.

Something else that is fun for correspondence is to write a postcard. Cut it up like a puzzle, put it in an envelope, and mail it. Then the child has to put it together before he or she can read it.

Another idea is to send postcards of local points of interest from your area. A postcard of the lakes, downtown, parks, libraries, and tourist attractions will spark interest and give the child ideas of what he or she would like to see when they come to visit you. Even though living hundreds of miles away from your grandchild is disheartening, the above examples show how you can find unique bonding opportunities for corresponding with your grandchildren.

Autobiographical Letters
Your Legacy, One Story at a Time

In autobiographical letters we can share our life and build a portrait of ourselves. This is legacy writing. Here is how this type of letter evolved for me.

After returning home from a vacation, I did the usual: I began to write a letter to my granddaughter sharing all the splendor of the trip. But this trip was special because I had gone back to revisit a place where I had camped as a child. As I was writing the letter, I realized that I really wanted to share the first time I had been there. I knew that story would be much more interesting to my granddaughter. So I described in as much detail as possible; the events, the adventures, and the feelings I had during that trip as a child and concluded with how I felt about that place today. The letter was received with much delight, and my new autobiographical letters were born. I found that my grandchildren loved the stories about my "olden days" and I was more than delighted to share them.

Letter to Megan, who was probably around five years old:

Dearest Beloved,

I have returned from my short vacation, although it seems it was an eternity away from you!

My poor car is still in the shop, so thank goodness I have a friend who does all the driving! Otherwise I would have to ride my bike. Imagine going on vacation on a bicycle!
That reminds me of a place I visited.

Many years ago (something like 40 long years ago), when I was just a little girl, like you Megan, (actually I was about 10), my family went camping. We had <u>eleven children</u> in our family, so we couldn't afford to go anywhere else for vacation. So, we always went camping. Well, this one year we went camping to a place called Gold Head Branch. It had a wonderful swimming lake.

What does one do when there are two girls trying to get to a swimming hole and there is only one bicycle upon which to ride? Have you an answer? YES! One girl tows the other on the back of the bike. And so I proceeded to tow my sister, Sarah. She didn't want me to do the towing because I was much smaller than her, and I wasn't as strong as her. But after much whining and bickering, she relented. So down the hill, to the swimming hole, we continued. We went fast! We went faster! We went so fast that the pedals turned much faster than my feet could go. Every time I tried to put my feet back on the pedals, the pedals would slap my feet and that HURT! So, I just stuck my feet straight out to the sides of the bike and let the bike fly down the hill, much like a bullet!

Poor Sarah on the back of the bike was screaming, "Stop the bike! Stop the bike!" Well, we were nearly to the swimming hole and I spotted a big wooden sign that said, "Swimming Ahead". I knew we were going to zoom right into the lake. I couldn't let that happen. So, I zoomed right into the sign, instead. Yes, we crashed into the sign and collapsed into a bruised and bloody heap. That was the only way I could stop the bike. All kinds of people ran over to see if we were OK. We were quite fine, except we were quite shaken (especially Sarah, she was LIVID)<*very mad*>. Remember, she didn't want me to tow her in the first place. She wanted to tow me.

Well, we picked ourselves up, cleaned up our cuts and bruises and went on to have a wonderful time swimming, camping, and playing. I will never forget the fabulous adventures at Gold Head Branch.

So, as I was saying early on, this last week I finally got to go back to Gold Head Branch (40 years later). I got to revisit the site of the bicycle crash. Would you believe the lake is still there? (however, since Florida is in a drought, it's nearly dried up, it's sort of a big mud hole now.) I did go fishing in that mud hole and ended up with my whole back covered in mud, but that's another story. Would you believe the same sign is there? So, as I was saying, 40 years later, I went back to Gold Head, saw the same swimming hole, saw the same sign, and even rode my bike again down the same hill. But this time I didn't crash!

I wish so much that you could accompany me on some of my trips. Perhaps one day. Until then, I will continue sending you postcards and telling you long stories, as grandmothers seem to like to do.

I hope you are still enjoying your new house. I hope your Mommy and Daddy aren't working too hard. I know they never stop working. I hope you and Hannah and Annabelle are having a good time swimming and playing. By the way, I keep wondering, does Annabelle swim in your pool? I hope I get to see you very soon because I miss you!

With all my love,XXXXOOOO

Curly Grandma

When we write autobiographical letters, we reveal how we perceived our place in life and in our family. We tell the story about when we were growing up—what it was like for us as kids. We tell stories that show what kind of family we had, what kind of home we lived in, what kind of school, church, and clubs we attended. We give our grandkids an idea of how different life was when we were little: no computers, no air-conditioning for a lot of us, and no Wal-Mart. We should give them an idea of how much the economy has changed: minimum wage was about eighty cents an hour, clotheslines were quite common, chicken was twenty-five cents a pound, shoes were bought only at shoe stores or major department stores, and catalogs were a major retail outlet for some rural areas. We will also want to explain how our town has changed: neighborhoods are gone, houses have been moved, and overpasses now sail over our swimming holes.

In autobiographical letters, you need to hone in on one moment in time, as you remember it, and explain what it was like for you. Do not worry if you do not remember it exactly as it was, because none of us ever remember the same situation in the same way. Just tell it as you remember it and don't worry. This is your story.

Most important to autobiographical letters are historical details. The tiniest pieces of information that you know and take for granted will be lost forever when you are gone. So, you must go out of your way to include such details as why you moved, who lived with you (for example, grandparents, cousins or foster children), where you attended church, school, and clubs, or even when siblings left home. Identify friends and neighbors, (it is surprising how many of these faces pop up in old photos and are mistaken for relatives) explain the family occupations and financial state of affairs if applicable, political or religious background, and any details that may seem unimportant but actually tie together the family history.

Plan ahead by recording some vital statistics, and incorporate them when possible. If you mention some of these facts in a letter, then you can refer back to that letter in subsequent correspondence rather than specifying the details again. An example would be: "Do you remember in my Thanksgiving letter how I told you about Uncle Jim who lived with us in 1953?"

> For the benefit of future generations be specific. Give the following:
> - Full names
> - Occupations
> - Dates, days, months and years
> - Relationships to other people mentioned in the letter
> - Ages, as often as possible
> - Full addresses; include city, state, and zip when possible
> - Names of churches, schools, and so forth; and give locations

Your letters do not have to be written in chronological order. In other words, you do not have to worry about starting at your birth and progressing to your adult life. You can pick a story from any time in your life and tell that story in a letter. It's as simple as that!

Each and every one of us has a lifetime of stories to share. But, there is no doubt; nearly all of us feel that we lack the talent, the expertise, or even the simple know-how to write our life experiences. We think that we are no good at grammar or spelling, and we never mastered all those important steps of composition. We want to write, we just can't. If that is how you feel, take comfort in the fact that many of us feel that way, and we must just do it! The riches of a literary jewel are at your fingertips. You need only to fashion it with pen and paper.

> The letters of a person…
> form the only full and genuine journal of his life.
> Thomas Jefferson (1743–1826)
> US diplomat, politician, and scholar; wrote Declaration of Independence 1776; 1st Secretary of State 1789–1793; vice-president of US 1797–1801; 3rd president of the US 1801- 1809

Sample Autobiographical Letters

The following autobiographical letter was written for Hannah Marie, an early second grader who was around seven years old, and it correctly includes an address for Hannah's future reference. My hope is that one day when Hannah is an adult, she will still have these letters, and if she needs some details for her family history she can refer back to the letters for information. However, my mistake was not including the city, state, and zip code if possible, maybe even a rough explanation such as, "Our house was very close to the old fire department." These kinds of details are important because the area has changed so much that this address no longer exists.

Of course, I should have explained a little more about what a bungalow house looks like, or better yet, sent a picture of the house. I should have given a more precise time element such as, "This was around 1954. I was about four years old." I should have explained more about Keemom and Keebob (my grandmother and grandfather) for even though my children know who they are, my grandchildren will not.

You can read the first page of the letter as it was presented originally, and then read some corrections in a following text box. The corrections show how the letter should have been written to incorporate autobiographical details. The last three pages of the letter have been omitted.

Letter to seven-year-old Hannah:

My Sweetie, My Sweetie,

It has been a long time since last I saw you. Missing you is something I do all the time. It is quite hot here in Earleton. So today I will stay inside most of the afternoon. That gives me a chance to write you a letter.

I remember a long time ago when I was about four or five years old I was also very hot. I was living in my grandmother's house. My mother had only five children at that time: John, me, Sarah, Danielle, and Kathy. We were living with Keemom and Keebob at 1053 East Rose St. It was a little tiny bungalow house with a front porch. We kids would sit on the front porch in only our underpants. We didn't wear shoes. We didn't wear any clothes, just our underpants. I remember how much I enjoyed not wearing clothes because it was so hot. We would run in and out of the house. We would run in and out of the screen door. We would slam the door each time. Mom or Keemom or Keebob would yell at us each time to stop slamming the door. We would still run in and out of the screen door slamming it each time. We didn't mean to. But we did. Slam, slam, slam.

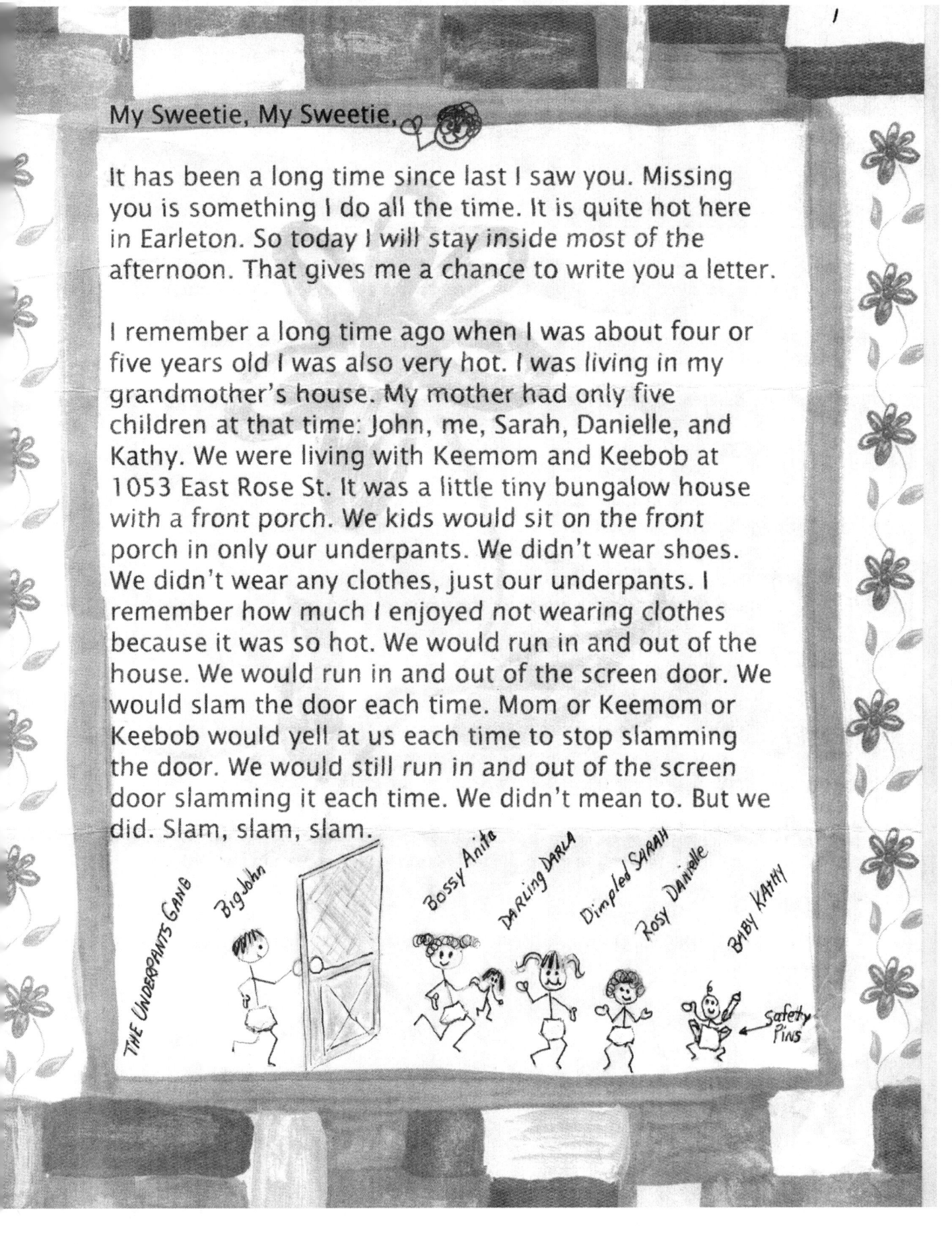

For employing good details, the beginning of Hannah's letter should have read something like this:

> I remember a long time ago when I was about four or five years old, around 1954, it was also very hot. My family was living with my grandparents, Keemom and Keebob. (Do you remember from my other stories that their real names are Carmel and John Sandella?) My mother, Vera Lou Budd Lewis, had only five children at that time: John, me (Anita), Sarah, Danielle, and Kathy.
>
> We were living with our grandparents, Keemom and Keebob, because my mother was very poor. My father had died, and my mother moved us out of the snow in Ashtabula, Ohio, down to the warm sun in Florida. You see, Hannah, buying snowsuits and snow boots for five children is very expensive; therefore, Keemom and Keebob let us live in their house for a while. We lived at 1053 E. Rose St., Lakeland, Florida. There were no zip codes back then, but that area today is in the 33805 area. We lived in a tiny little Craftsman bungalow house with a front porch. A bungalow is a little square house with a porch all the way across the front, and the porch usually has nice big fat steps and big fat pillars (posts).

The above information will be crucial to future generations. I was very surprised to learn from conversation that even my own children were not sure of legal and maiden names of their great-grandparents. Consequently, if I am writing to my grandchildren, they certainly will not know this information about Keemom and Keebob unless I document it frequently.

Reminding Hannah of our financial condition when we moved to Florida is not only interesting, it also helps Hannah to grasp the real reason we ran around in our underwear all the time: poverty.

Another technique for making this letter fun and enticing was attention to illustrations. I painted the kids' underwear with white-out to make them "pop" out of the picture. This letter was sure to "stick" in Hannah's mind.

> Here is a great idea to introduce grandchildren to their ancestors:
> - Scan an old photo of a great, great grandparent or other relative, who is long gone.
> - Paste it into a word document.
> - Write all you know about that relative.
> - Because this is a letter, include stories of personal interaction you may have had with this ancestor or any personal comments. If you are not confident about the details, go ahead and include them, but be sure to specify something like, "I don't know for sure, but I think … "
> - Include anything that others have told you, such as, "Uncle Wendell once said…"
> - Also include any biographical details: legal names, addresses, dates, relation, marriages, age in photo, offspring, financial situations, even pets or friends.

Breathe life into old photos and resurrect those long-lost faces from dusty, mildewy albums. In doing so, you will leave your descendents a clear and personal image of their ancestors. The following letter to Megan, a 13 year old, is an example of how I have used this idea. The letter has been inserted with no stationery, decorations, or signature.

Dearest Beloved,

How have you been?

   I so wish that I had something great to write about. I wish that I could write about some great adventurous event in my life. But, I have absolutely nothing to write about. So, I got to looking around and going through my old photo albums. And guess what? I found something to write about. I found some really good pictures.

   Your Aunt Sarah, my sister in Mississippi. was here, and we were going through some family history. Well, I got hold of some really old photos.

   Do you remember your 4 X great grandmother that I told you about? I know your mind is just a churnin.' I know your thinking, "Curly Grandma, how do I possibly remember her?" Well, now you don't have to remember. I will tell you, and, better yet, I'll show you.

   Here she is: Your maternal Great-Great-Great-Great- Grandmother

This is Anna Werner Ellers Meyers

We don't know when she was born or when she died. We think this picture was taken somewhere around 1937.

We don't know exactly what her maiden name is: either Werner or Warner. Anyway, we found out some good stuff. She was married to an artist. Mr. Ellers. That would make her name Anna Werner Ellers. But, something happened, and he disappeared. So she married again. She married Mr. Celestine Meyers. Here is a picture of him. So, now her name is Anna Werner Ellers Meyers.

Now, here is an interesting part: although we don't know their dates of birth or death, we think they were marrying somewhere around the 1890's. So, when you watch TV and you see movies about our country, The Union and The Confederate armies fighting over slavery, think about your Grandma and Grandpa Meyers who were very young children at that time.

When Anna Meyers married Celestine Meyers, they lived in Pittston, Pennsylvania. They ran a grocery store. They lived upstairs and the store was downstairs. Here is a great photo of that little store.

You can't read the signs scattered all around the windows and on the wall, but I put the photo in my scanner and made the picture big so I could read some of them. A few of them say things like:

GROCERIES

CIGARS. CANDIES
TOBACCO & CIGARS
HAVANNAH RIBBON

SEEDS

10 CENTS / PACKAGE
OL—WAGON SOAP
MAGIC YEAST

FLEISCHMAN'S YEAST

It seems to me that cigars were a pretty popular item to sell in stores back then. Something else they must have sold a lot of, was flour, sugar and other baking goods. Yeast is the ingredient in bread that makes it rise. Most people baked their own bread back then, so yeast must have been a popular item. I love the "wagon soap" sign. Just think, soap to wash your wagons?

My mother, Vera Lewis, your Grandma Lewis, said that she remembers the Meyers still had their store when she was very young. She remembers getting some candy from the store. She doesn't remember getting it often. It was a treat. My mother also said she remembers Grandma Meyers as being very sweet. Grandma Meyers was my mother's great-grandmother, so she was already very old when my mother knew her.

My mother said she remembered Grandpa Meyers as being very quiet, but that she wasn't around the "men folk" much and so she didn't get much of a chance to know him.

Back in the old days, the men didn't spend much time with the kids. The children stayed around the women and were told not to bother the men, because the men were always working. Things are different today. Aren't you glad?

Something else that was very different back in the old days is that photographs weren't common. People didn't own cameras, and so no one could take pictures of their family. If you wanted a picture of your family, it was very expensive, and you had to go to a photographer's shop or you had to get the photographer to come to your house. Usually, in the old days the photos were printed on something like a postcard. On the back of this store picture, it says POSTCARD. Most of my old family photos from the 1800's say POSTCARD on the back. Obviously the photographer came to the store to take this picture, and you can see that our grandparents are all spiffed up in their good duds for this occasion.

The next picture is on the very same POSTCARD paper as the store.

So, we are sure that the lady sitting down is Grandma Meyers; the face looks exactly the same when the picture is blown up on a scanner. Boy, did she get dressed up for this sitting! Boy, oh boy, she wanted to look like quite a lady. We think this picture was taken in the early 1900's, just like the store photo.

Megan, can you imagine what she was thinking as she sat for this picture? Don't you know that she was thinking maybe one day her great-great grandchildren would want to know about her? I bet she never even thought her 4Xgreat grandchildren would ever see her photo. Don't you wish we had some letters from her? Don't you wish we could just go back in time and ask her all kinds of questions about her life as a child, about her horses, about her lost husband, about everything? I look at her photo and I just wonder. I wonder all these things, and I wonder if one day my great-great-great-great-great grandchildren will say, "Wow, look at all these letters. This is my Gx5 grandmother!"

This last photo is the Meyers in a 1912 automobile. Isn't this the coolest photo?

I can't imagine how expensive a car was back then. We are not exactly sure that they are in the photo. But we know the lady in the back is Maud Ellers Stroup, daughter of Anna Ellers Meyers. The girls are Maud's daughters, Carmel and Erma Stroup. Carmel Stroup Sandella is your Keemom, your -great-great grandmother. Pretty cool, huh?

Well, I guess I must go now; I have been putting off doing my housework, lately. I think the summer heat makes me lazy. I should be cleaning all my bathrooms, and washing clothes, and pulling weeds, but I am too lazy. I would rather write to you about old pictures. I think I will go find some more photos!

Love, and thinking of you always,
Curly Grandma

Be sure to hole-punch your letter, and get it ready for the notebook, (the notebook is discussed in *Chapter 2: The Cycle of Correspondence*) just as you will do with all of your letters. You do not want your letters to get lost.

The above letter is important because family albums get passed on to only one person who then passes it on to only his immediate family. Other family members usually lose out on the opportunity of owning old family photos; they may never even know the albums exist; or worse, the albums get split up with no information to match the photos. Therefore, if you can get these photos and your stories to match now, and get them out to all of your grandchildren now, their heritage will not be lost and there will be references for many, rather than one.

You have so many long lasting relationships and they make wonderful stories. You should get them down on paper. Why not pull out school yearbooks, old photo albums, and even old diaries to sift through and jot down meaningful experiences that can be shared in a letter? A good idea is to keep a running list of stories. Cross off the ones you use and keep adding new stories. If a computer is one of your tools, identify the file name of each letter with a name, date, and a quick title description, such as M.Meyers.1–07 for the above letter. Try making a simple chart of experiences that bring back good memories. Jot down ideas for letters. The following chart is my beginning: Each entry is a new letter, possibly more than one.

MEMORIES:

SCHOOL	Walk to and from school	Elk's Club	Slide down hill
HOMEWORK	Hours and hours!	Call at telephone booth to ask someone if I forget	
CHURCH	Church every morning before school	Sunday afternoon fried chicken-DISHES	
BED TIME	One room for nine girls Three bunk beds	Dad builds a "dormitory"	
BATH TIME	Recycled towels Share water	4 babies in the tub, Dad first then Mom, then kids	
PLAY TIME	Skate, hop scotch, cement in backyard	Skate down road with baby on hip	Ice-cream at Jimbo's
LAUNDRY	Hang up diapers every day after school (rain)	No dryer, clothesline	Mountain on the couch
VACATION	Camping Gold-Head Branch	Oleno- plug in fan Bad water	Ashtabula, Ohio
SEASONS	No air-cond:HOT No insulation:Cold	One gas heater- brittle hair	Hurricanes
TV	MitchMiller/Mickey Mouse Club	Friday nights-*Man from Uncle*/make fudge	
MEALS	Saturday house clean- P-nut Butter/Jelly	Jello-pound cake Sit on the curb and eat it	Skillet dinners, chili,
CHORES	Starch & iron uniforms	Rotate five jobs- clear, wash, dry, put-away, sweep	Wash baby diapers
RELATIVES	Aunt Dorthea Keemom, Keebob	Grandma Lewis, Melba, Wendel, Linda, Ike,	Gerri, Bucky, Skippy
CARS	"Nelly Bell" Mom-no license	Many station wagons	
SHOPPING	Walk home with eitht boxes ice cream before it melts	No Walmart- Penny's Pay tubes, McCrory's	Quick Check-walk with baby buggy, play carts on Sunday
	Wednesday was pay day Bags & Bags	Made hamburgers on grocery night YUM!	Only two kids could go. Took turns

Keep in mind that the "good ol' days" are extremely interesting to grandchildren, but your life today is just as significant, just as interesting, and in some ways more aligned with their current concerns. Your everyday activities make for some very inspiring stories that riddle a letter with fun and intrigue. Therefore, both kinds of letters, friendly and autobiographical, are well appreciated by grandchildren. The only thing that really matters is that you pick up the pen or sit at your computer and write! That way you officially become an inkslinger and through each letter, you build your legacy. Most of all, your grandchildren will be looking forward to each of your letters and you are sure to become timeless!

> If you cannot get rid of the family skeleton,
> you may as well make it dance.
>
> George Bernard Shaw
> Irish dramatist & socialist (1856 - 1950)

Chapter 2

The Cycle of Correspondence

Corresponding with grandchildren is fun and rewarding. Adding a few steps can turn your letters into a memoir or autobiography. This chapter explains how to assemble and save your letters and how you can organize the topics in your letters. Let's begin with how the cycle of correspondence plays out:

1. Write a letter to the grandchild.
2. Illustrate and decorate the letter.
3. Hole-punch the letter and place sticky reinforcers on the holes to prevent tearing.
4. Place the letter in a decorated envelope. Include a stamped, return envelope and stationery for the child's return letter. Pre-address the envelope for very young children or include address labels.
5. Optional: Include decorative stickers for the child's use.
6. Make a copy of your letter before mailing.
7. Mail the letter. Sit back and wait for a response letter, or get busy on the next one.
8. The child receives the letter, reads it, places it in their notebook (explained on the next page), writes a response letter on the enclosed paper, decorates it, places it in the stamped envelope, and mails it.
9. The grandparent receives the return letter and can't wait to write another!

This system manages the grandparent's letters and ensures that the child will have the materials for immediate response. If the child has to find his own paper, envelope and stamp, he may lose interest or get sidetracked. It could then take quite a while before the grandparent receives a letter, if one is received at all.

If you want to turn the envelope into a learning experience for school-age children, try the following steps:

> Children Younger than Five: Send a self-addressed return envelope.
> - Five- and Six-year-olds: Enclose address labels; write your name very lightly on the return envelope in the spot where the child should stick your address label. Write his name very lightly on the spot where he should write his address, or he can use Mom's address labels with help.
> - Seven- and Eight-year-olds: Cut the address labels into strips. They can look at the original envelope for guidance. Or you can handle it the same as for five-and six-year-olds.
> - Nine- and Ten-year-olds: Enclose blank labels, the child can write the addresses and decorate them.

The Notebook

Some form of notebook is paramount to the success of compiling our autobiography. Each of our letters is more than a letter; it is a hard copy of our efforts. We want our efforts to be taken care of, to be tended to, to be respected, and that is what the notebook does. This applies to both grandparent and grandchild.

When you begin correspondence, buy two notebooks; one for the child and one for yourself. One-inch, three-ring vinyl notebooks work well. Also, buy a three-hole paper punch and sticky hole-reinforcers. Hole-punch the letter and place the sticky reinforcements on the holes before you mail it. Otherwise the letters tear easily and may be lost.

When you give the notebook to the child, explain that you want him to save your letters in the notebook, and you have one just like it for saving his letters. Tell him that when you visit him, you can go through the old letters together, read them and find his favorite, the funniest, the one with the best illustrations, and so forth. Revisiting these letters in the notebook is fun and it helps the grandparent see what the child likes best for future letters.

Make copies of your letters before you mail them because if you are saving your letters on a computer, the file contains only text; it will not have illustrations. Luckily, most post offices have a copy machine available to customers, and you can copy the illustrated letter for your files just before you pop it into the envelope.

Why do you even need a copy of the letter you are sending to the child? Because children lose things—they lose a lot of things, all the time. They will definitely lose your letters. One day, in a far, far away time, you will want your letter collection to be complete. Sorry, but you can not depend on children to accomplish this long-term goal. They are not capable. If you are very lucky, Mom or Dad might have all the letters intact, but just in case, keep a copy.

I wouldn't have known this except that my daughter, Shannan, told me when her girls got a letter from me they wanted to take it to school, share it with teachers and friends, carry it around in their backpack, and then save it somewhere in their room. Shannan always felt pressured to "rescue" the letter. She was worried it would disappear, forever! But, most of all, feeding horses, pigs, and dogs (not to mention kids and a husband), was getting in the way of saving letters! Shannan was relieved to find out I was keeping copies. A lot of pressure was lifted, she was able to relax, feed the animals and family, and let the girls enjoy their letters for as long as they wanted. Eventually, the letters showed up on the desk or under the bed and found their way to the notebook.

Another reason for copying the letters is that you need a copy. Believe it or not, you might forget what you have written about in past letters. You might forget who got what topic, and you may begin repeating some subjects. You may also want to split some topics into several letters, and you will need copies for coherency.

A simple chart such as the one illustrated below (either on the computer, or in a notebook) may help keep track of correspondence.

LETTERS		
MEGAN	**HANNAH**	**RILEY**
Mar 2001 Footprints	Mar 2001 Walk to school	5-24-04 (photos) Yellow house in trees
June 2001 Glow worm	Aug 2001 Crunching Hannah	6-16-04 Bang on jeep
9-6-01 Toothbrushes	Sept. 01 Xmas	7-22-04 Fix Swing

Another idea is for parents to make a copy of the child's letter before he mails it. Someday, the child will want to pass on his letters as part of the family history.

One might wonder, "Why even give a notebook to the child if we are keeping copies before we mail them?" The answer is that the child needs to have an active part in this process. What makes this project work is a special connection between grandparent and child. This connection is structured with elements such as engaging in a common project, embracing each other's personal efforts, gaining profound insight into each other's character, and recognizing and appreciating the enduring interest and attention demonstrated in correspondence. So the child must have their notebook to validate their partnership in this project.

Now that we have seen how important the notebook is, I have to share another thought. My daughter, Shannan, explained to me that once I started decorating envelopes, my granddaughters thought the envelopes were too pretty to throw away, and saving the letters in a notebook became a problem. They started keeping the letters, still in the envelopes, in a photo box. Photo boxes were filled quickly and the girls went to large organizational boxes. I solved the problem by hole-punching the envelopes along the bottom edge so the girls could keep the letters and the envelopes together in a notebook.

How the child saves his or her letters becomes a matter individual to each family. The important thing is that the child is given a convenient method for collecting his letters so that he is able to carry on his end of the relationship. Therefore, choose a notebook, a box, a basket, or even a drawer. Just choose a method that works easily for the child but also safeguards the letter and is comfortable for the whole family.

One last idea for saving letters is to put them in photo sleeves—clear plastic sleeves (some are acid-free). They already have the holes for the notebook. In super stores they can be found in photo or scrap-booking sections or in the stationery department.

> I have made this [letter] longer,
> because I have not had the time to make it shorter.
>
> Blaise Pascal "Lettres Provincials," letter 16, 1657
> French mathematician, physicist (1623–1662)

Chapter 3

The Heart of Correspondence

Few people write personal letters today. That's a shame. Such correspondence lends an air of endowment to the recipient, especially to a child. Receiving a letter means somebody took personal time to write down their special thoughts and then send them as tangible proof of their love and concern. This is the heart of correspondence—emotions in black and white, feelings in print revealed and exchanged by two people. We take a risk when we put words on paper, and so the heart must rule this peril.

Children are thrilled when they receive a letter! They view letters as significant because they do not think of themselves as important in the family (as autonomous) and to children, mail is for the important people in the family. Most children know they are important to their parents, but they do not see themselves as important. Their very existence has no sovereignty; they belong to Mommy and Daddy. To them, the family unit is a vehicle to get them through each day. There is no plan in their life. There is just the home, the school, the babysitter, the TV, and so forth. To a child, receiving a letter demonstrates and validates his or her importance in the family and in life in general.

Visualize a preschooler watching the parent open mail; mostly bills, of course. The parent is very intent on reading and studying and probably even emits messages of "Not now" or "Later, please" to the child while reading. The child knows mail is important because Mommy or Daddy becomes engrossed in it and essentially becomes detached from the child.

My granddaughter, Megan, put it in these words, "I like to get letters because every day Mommy gets the bills because she takes care of stuff." She went on to explain that she knew her parents were very important people because there was a lot of mail for them every day. She linked mail with importance. It is natural for children to make that assumption. Therefore, including them in the postal cadence integrates them into the life category of importance (at least as far as they are concerned).

For a child, the gift of a letter and the anticipation of a letter is as much fun as waiting for a special occasion. Even in school, children love to send and receive notes, and they will risk punishment to do so. This is correspondence on a smaller scale. Even so, it is just as important to the participants, and it accomplishes the goal of connecting to others, just like ordinary letter writing.

As a teacher, I have personally experienced the resolve children have in accomplishing this exchange: They will risk much and resort to shrewd and crafty behavior just to write to each other. But, it was when my own daughter, Shannan, was in high school that I first realized just how important correspondence is. I discovered a small laundry basket filled with years of notes (neatly folded into origami-like shapes) stuffed under her bed. Her notes were to, and from, friends, teachers, coaches, and all the people who touched her life throughout school. The notes chronicled the change and growth of my little girl. It was touching to read her actual feelings during those school years. And, I am surprised that such a good student could have participated in such voluminous correspondence. She, of course, tossed them in the trash. Today, I wish I had those notes.

> Words have a longer life than deeds.
> Pindar, Nemean Odes
> Greek lyric poet (522 BC - 433 BC)

When you begin your long-term correspondence with grandchildren, you should keep in mind three very basic principles or rules.

THREE RULES

1.	2.	3.
Write	Illustrate or Decorate	Make Your Correspondence Free

Rule #1: Write!

Write. Just write. Do not pay attention to spelling or punctuation because you cannot create if you are editing. So just let the thoughts spill out onto the paper. It is difficult at first, but make yourself write quickly, abbreviating as much as you can without losing readability. This is easiest on a word processor or computer. The important thing is that you write! Yes, you can go back and rewrite your letter with improved spelling and punctuation before you mail it. But remember—this is a letter. It is not a recorded instrument for county records: it is not a will and testament—it is a letter. Regardless of what your sixth-grade teacher told you, it can have mistakes and still be a perfectly fine letter. Some of the letters in this book qualify as downright offensive when it comes to good grammar! If Curly Grandma is willing to put these blunders in a book, that should give you all the courage necessary to send letters with grammatical misdemeanors.

However, if you are still apprehensive because your grandchild is a flowering scholar, you might want to ask him or her to edit your letter and write an explanation of each mistake and provide its corrected form. Example: "Johnny, I have some hidden errors in this letter. If you are looking for something to do, you can find all the errors and provide the corrections to me."

I promise you, most of our grandchildren will not be searching for tasks of this nature. And again, punctuation, capitalization, and sentence structure are not of urgent matters when reading our correspondence. So, just write!

Now, in spite of everything mentioned above, if you still remain reluctant to mail letters with composition flaws, one last recommendation that may provide immense help is a sixth grade Language Arts book—a grammar book. Almost certainly, even a fourth or fifth grade English book will do (not a literature book because it will focus on stories, essays, poetry, and other such literature). You want to be sure to get a book that explains grammar and usage. You might even want to get a Teacher's Edition; it has all the answers in it. That's really helpful! Some county school boards will let the public pick up discontinued books for free at the warehouse at least one day per month when they are open to the public. Call before you make the trip. My home county in Florida had such a system, but it was always wise to call first because the hours were short and inconsistent on many occasions. Many states purchase textbooks differently and offer no public access. Find out what your state and county policy is.

Another way to secure an English textbook is on the Internet. It should be pretty easy to purchase used books through eBay or Amazon. Additionally, do not forget about the neighborhood used bookstores.

A sixth grade English book is a good choice because it contains all the basics. It is easy to understand, it explains grammar, usage, and punctuation complexities; it shows most of the common mistakes; it has many examples, and the index is an easy one to consult. It also has some great literature in it, and you can pilfer ideas to style your language. For example, you might like the way an author repeats something over and over, and so you might do it in your letter. So, if I find myself really questioning my grammar, usage, or punctuation to the point that I cannot sleep, I go to my sixth grade book. But, again, keep in mind that the grammar, usage, and parts of a friendly letter are secondary to the basic elements of content and emotional exchange. True correspondence is genuine and key even when the content is mechanically or grammatically flawed. If only editors could reach out and thrash me for that statement! They would be a happy lot!

Another book you will find helpful is the thesaurus. Thank goodness our computer has the good ol' speller and thesaurus in the tool bar. My procedure is to write the whole letter on the computer and then have fun. I read each sentence and each time I find an ol' humdrum word I zap it with a replacement adjective from the thesaurus. I then reconfigure my words. Ta da! Here is a simple example of how it might work.

We were <u>poor</u> little <u>kids</u> with a <u>lot of work</u> to do every day. *(my words)*

What an <u>underprivileged brood</u> we were, with <u>numerous, unpleasant chores</u> ahead of us each and every day. *(not my typical language, you can tell, right?)*

Not only is it fun to do this, but our grandchildren will love to read the new words. Big, new, or unusual words are a delight to children. The explanation must lie somewhere in the kind of parroting we find in a typical three-year-old child, such as my grandson, Riley. He walks around reciting in a choppy tone, "It is forbidden, it is forbidden" as though he is reciting a rhyme or poem. He may not have a real grasp of that word, but he loves the sound of it, and I guess he likes the way it rolls off his tongue. I guess children like the way big new words chime a resounding tone.

We all have this gift of rhythm. We all have this gift of "letter gab." It is embedded in our brains; we have to find it, drag it out, fine tune it with practice, such as writing letter after letter, and put it out front where we can see it…rather, use it. After a few letters, you will become very comfortable with writing a first draft that can be mailed. Each of you will quickly develop your own style and techniques.

Picture this: A child is playing on the floor while her mother is sitting at the table with a friend, gabbing and conversing about everyday things. The child is listening, but she is not really engaged in what the adults are saying. What she is paying attention to is the melody of their language and the synchronization of tone and dialect. The conversation consumes the child. The important thing that is happening is that the language transaction is basically downloading an operating system into the child's brain. As with all young children, the child is recording their conversation into a hard-wired format for future talking, reading, and writing skills. We all have this hard drive. We all have this flow of language. We just have to use it, and the more we write letters, the better we develop it and the easier language flows.

Now that I have exhausted several paragraphs telling you how unessential perfect grammar and usage is in correspondence, I must interject: children copy and repeat our methods and techniques. They do as they see and hear. Therefore, we have a responsibility to do the best we can without being sloppy or careless. We do not want to teach or reinforce mistakes and bad habits.

The following letter to seven-year-old Megan (a good reader at this age), is a good example of how I try to let language flow as if I were talking to her. The letter is filled with new and challenging words, but I used the rhythm of the story to explain these words. This letter is probably too difficult for an early seven-year-old, but not for a child who is nearly eight. Megan may have come upon a word that she didn't know, but if she kept on reading she would get the explanation, or more importantly the "feeling" of the word. Many times I defined with parenthesis or pattern, but I tried to depend on the natural flow of the language to help her comprehend.

Another strong point of this letter is how well the illustrations support the text. All through the letter, the comments, drawings, and stickers clarify what the text is saying to the child. In Chapter 6: Target Your Audience, we will see how important this is for young children.

Luckily, this letter also allows you to see what not to do. While reading, you will notice that many of the paragraphs are formatted incorrectly: they are too long, and they include too many thoughts and sentences. Good readers will have no problem with this, but a struggling reader could be challenged. Spelling and punctuation is not perfect in the following letter, but it is not distracting; it is a great letter for friendly correspondence.

A little background information about this letter may help. Megan is my oldest grandchild and I address her as "Dearest Beloved." She was living in Ft. Meade, Florida at the time of this writing. Her family had just moved to the countryside and was busy ranching. Riley (six months old) is her cousin who lived in Gainesville, Florida, about three-and-a- half hours away. I had just moved near Gainesville, and I was Riley's babysitter while his parents were starting a business. And so, I kept Megan and Hannah updated on all the antics of Baby Riley. This letter was written when I had only three grandchildren; Megan and Hannah, who are sisters, and Riley.

Letter to seven-and-a-half-year-old Megan:

August 17, 2001 (or thereabouts)

Dearest Beloved,

I haven't too much to say today. I could begin with the usual "*stuff*" about how much I miss you. I *could* tell you how I am simply miserable in being so far away from you. However, because I just left you a few days ago, your image and your aura (that means your face and your love) are still with me. So, I shall not go *on and on* with my usual *lamenting* (that means whining and crying).

I want to tell you how much I enjoyed my visit Saturday. Watching you ride Beauty was a spectacular thing. You are certainly a natural rider. You sit up in the saddle so tall. And you take command of your pony so professionally. It was quite a sight to see my little granddaughter *displaying such a unique talent* (that means showing such a special talent). I hope you will also tell your Mommy that I was immensely impressed with her capabilities. She certainly picked up equestrian techniques very quickly. I think your Mommy and Daddy are very impressive to watch. Maybe I am just too easy to impress, but I don't think so.

I am staying very busy with Riley lately. Aunt Angie has to work a lot of extra hours and so she is away from home quite a bit. That means that I shall have to look after the baby while she is away. It makes me very happy that I can take care of him instead of a stranger or just a regular hired baby sitter. You know, Megan, I think family members make the best baby sitters because they love the baby. Don't you think that is true?

Riley is quite fun. He likes to push the buttons on his miniature SEE AND SAY and make kitty sounds (well he doesn't actually push the buttons, he sort of pounds them or bashes them because he doesn't have good finger use, you know). He doesn't know it's a kitty sound. He doesn't even know what a kitty is. But he hears the kitty sound and repeats it back. If *you* were to hear him make a kitty sound, you wouldn't even know it was a kitty sound. He just sort of makes a light, little *ahhhhhh*. But, *I* know it's a kitty sound. It's a funny thing about Riley. His kitty sound, his horsy sound, his piggy sound, his lamb sound.... They all sound the same. But the important thing is that he makes a sound after the SEE AND SAY makes a sound. And so that is what this Curly Grandma spends hours doing: watching Riley make some kind of sound. Any sound will do. All his sounds are special.

This reminds me of a time when you were just about Riley's age, about five months old. I think I shall tell a tale of "Megan the Glow Worm".

We took you to the Crystal Springs Beach for a weekend. *It's very difficult to take small babies to the beach because they get so miserable from not enough rest, missing their beds, different foods; you can just imagine what could make a baby miserable, right?* Let's continue with "Megan the Glow Worm". Well, you were so good and so cute. The days were very hot and we made sure you were safely shielded from the sun. The nights were comfortable and we wrapped you in a light blanket and pushed you around in an umbrella stroller (that's a stroller like your doll buggy, if you recall, one that folds up like an umbrella). We called you our little *GlowWorm* because you sat in the buggy, all cocooned in a tight little blanket, smiling and glowing for every person who stopped to look at you and comment about how good you were. Well, you *were* good. And you certainly appeared very happy.

However, (you know something is changing after that word *however*, don't you?) Well, I suppose you had had enough of the beach sooner than we expected. For, on the way home in the car, you commenced to screaming. **Screaming loudly.** I should say **screaming very loudly.** Your screaming came about so suddenly that we all thought you had been bitten by a bug, or stuck by a pin, or perhaps you had suddenly taken ill by some fatal, immediate disease. All of us grownups frantically passed you back and forth, each of us sure that we knew the secret to pacifying you. We all looked at each other in amazement and puzzlement. For **you**, Megan, and don't forget you were only five months old, probably only about 12 pounds, and probably only having 1 or 2 teeth, certainly not a commanding human being at this time; **you** had succeeded in turning all of us grownups into a MANGLE OF FRETTING CARETAKERS. You were a ball of CONTAGIOUS FRENZY!

We stopped to eat in a restaurant because we were all hungry, but you *relentlessly* continued screaming. Your poor Daddy, he had to stay outside and walk you about, bouncing you on his shoulder hoping to quiet you. I don't recall if he ever got a bite to eat (or was that your poor Mommy?). Finally, if my memory serves me right, you stopped as suddenly as you had started. And none of us grownups ever figured out the mystery of the crying *GlowWorm*. But I do think it was quite a *long time* before we ever took you on another long trip!

Well, I must go now. I must go and wash my very dirty and very smelly clothes, because I take Riley for a walk every day and I jog while I push him in the buggy, and so I smell like a *dish rag or perhaps an old sponge* when I get back to the house (from all that sweat, you know). And so you can imagine how my clothes smell.

Well goodbye, My Dearest. Have lots of fun at school. Don't let your friends treat you badly, and you treat them nicely. Play kindly with Hannah; pet your wonderful animals for me. Give your wonderful Mommy and Daddy a big hug for me. And remember your *guardian angel* is always watching out for you, so have fun in everything you do.

I miss you. I love you. I think of you always.

Love,

Curly Grandma

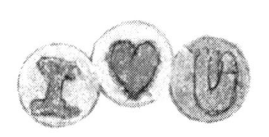

GAGA
That means FASTER!

Why is the sun always hottest when I'm jogging? or is it?

Stationery

Choice of stationery is a personal matter, but a few points to ponder may help. The stationery in the previous letter is a good choice for a young child because it has a tight, colorful border. The solid white background is perfect to allow illustrations to pop out at the child, and there is plenty of room for the drawings. Many of my first letters to my grandchildren were on very busy, colorful stationery, and the illustrations would get lost and lose their impact. When your message is in the pictures you want nothing to distract from them, so your best choice would be plain white paper.

Pastel paper is fine for young children as long as it has a tight border (one that is narrow and stays tightly to the edge of the paper). On some stationery we will find loose borders (the border is wide and not well defined, and the decorations or images in the border flow out into the writing area). This can be distracting to a young reader, but older children have no problem with it. If your grandchild has a learning disability of some sort, busy paper is highly distracting to him. Plain, white paper is always the better choice for this child.

The determining factors in choosing stationery are if the letter is to be read aloud or if the letter is for an independent reader. Letters to be read aloud are much more forgiving because the parent will help the child to make sense of the text and illustrations.

Here are a few suggestions that may help:

Age	Stationery
Infants	It does not matter what you use.
1, 2, 3	Use white or plain pastels. Use tight borders.
4, 5	Use white or light pastels.
	Tight borders are best, but loose borders are fine if the colors are soft.
	Color your drawings with the same colors in the border for less distraction.
6, 7, 8	Use plain white or pastel paper if you are going to have margin messages, wandering illustrations, numerous stickers, or very bright colors in your illustrations.
	Bright colorful stationery with loose borders can work if you keep the print and illustrations away from the border.
	Coloring your illustrations with the same colors in the border helps to minimize distraction.
9 *and up*	It does not matter.
	(good readers)

Rule #2: Illustrate or Decorate

Every letter should contain illustrations or at least some kind of colorful decoration. Sometimes, personal and colorful stationery is enough. Someone said it best long, long ago: "A picture is worth a thousand words." Children do not tire of illustrations, thus the more, the better. You do not have to be a great artist. You need only to be able to draw the simple little stickmen that first and second graders use; the more primitive the drawings are, the more fun the letter is. Stick figures allow the child to imagine the fine details. I have found that upon receiving a letter, my grandchildren may even add some of their own details to my pictures.

You may want to try exaggerating the main topic in the picture. For example, if the picture depicts you on a bike, make the wheels very big, or if you are writing about a phone conversation, make the phone stand out in some way, such as size or color.

Kids are very forgiving of artistic shortcomings. They do not have the perspective that adults do, and so they are not the critics we think they are. Hence, we should not be afraid to illustrate. Besides, if our pictures are not great, that means when a child writes his return letter, the stress of performing perfectly is lifted. Be sure to include at least one illustration on each page. If you have no time to illustrate, decorate with stickers or stamps. It is easiest if you first draw your pictures in pencil and then color with crayons, colored pencils, or markers. How about those sparkle pens or metallic gels? Anything will do!

Remember that you must leave some empty space for your drawings. On a computer, press enter six to ten times and that will give you plenty of room.

When I draw my figures, I begin with a simple stick figure.

The second thing I do is draw some kind of clothing over the figure. Children seem to love the clothing on the figures. I do not know why, but they do. A good guess would be that the clothes are the most colorful part, and so "the clothes do make the man," as the old saying goes.

Next, I erase the stick part of the figure that is inside the clothes.

Then I add details: shoes, socks, buttons, or any ornamentation. After that, I add details such as hair and facial expressions, even some kind of hands or fists. Do not bother with fingers.

Last, I color in the clothes and absolutely anything that can be colored, right down to raindrops or tears. If your picture does not look how it is supposed to look, that is okay. Do what I do—label it. I draw an arrow and write what it is. However, I think it is important that you include an adjective in the label. For instance, boiling pot is better than pot, or livid Sarah is better than Sarah. The more unusual the adjective, the better it works. This little technique enhances your grandchild's vocabulary, understanding, visualization, and perception.

When reading, a child gets the feeling of the message by reading words, but also by studying illustrations that accompany the print. The faces in our illustration deliver emotional impact. Facial expressions can clarify and highlight the emotion in the print. As a result, facial expressions are easily understood and appreciated by children.

As I began to draw faces, I figured out a little trick for down and out expressions: the eyes and mouth are positioned low on the face. Check out the sad, miserable, and disappointed expressions in the images on page 48. On the opposite spectrum, notice that the eyes and mouth are positioned up high on the face for emotions such as happy, content, and hopeful. Round eyes express alertness, but curvy or straight lines reveal an expression of looking inward to ourselves. The mouth tends to be wide and sometimes open for happy emotions, but small or turned down for negative.

The eyebrows are a feature that can be left out completely for most happy faces. But, notice how important they become for negative expressions. I learned a lot about eyebrows from my grandson, Riley. When he was about 18 months old, he would reach out and try to push his mother's eyebrows up if she was upset with him. One day, I watched my daughter, Angie, scolding Riley, now three years old; he was scowling, looking down and his arms were folded in a resentful tone. "You better get those eyebrows up when I'm talking to you, young man," Angie snapped. Riley immediately lifted his brows way up to the top of his head, and his mouth couldn't help but follow. His head turned up to his mother as his arms dropped down to his side. His facial expression and body language changed drastically. It wasn't completely from effort: He couldn't help but relax his mouth and arms when he lifted up his brows. I was amazed. I tried it. When I lifted my brows way up to the top of my head, I could feel positive emotions flowing in. So, don't underestimate eyebrows!

Having many faces to study and copy is extremely helpful when illustrating. Therefore the following images, simple as they are, should be a valuable resource. A little tweaking with these basic faces will generate almost any needed expression.

How does your drawing feel?

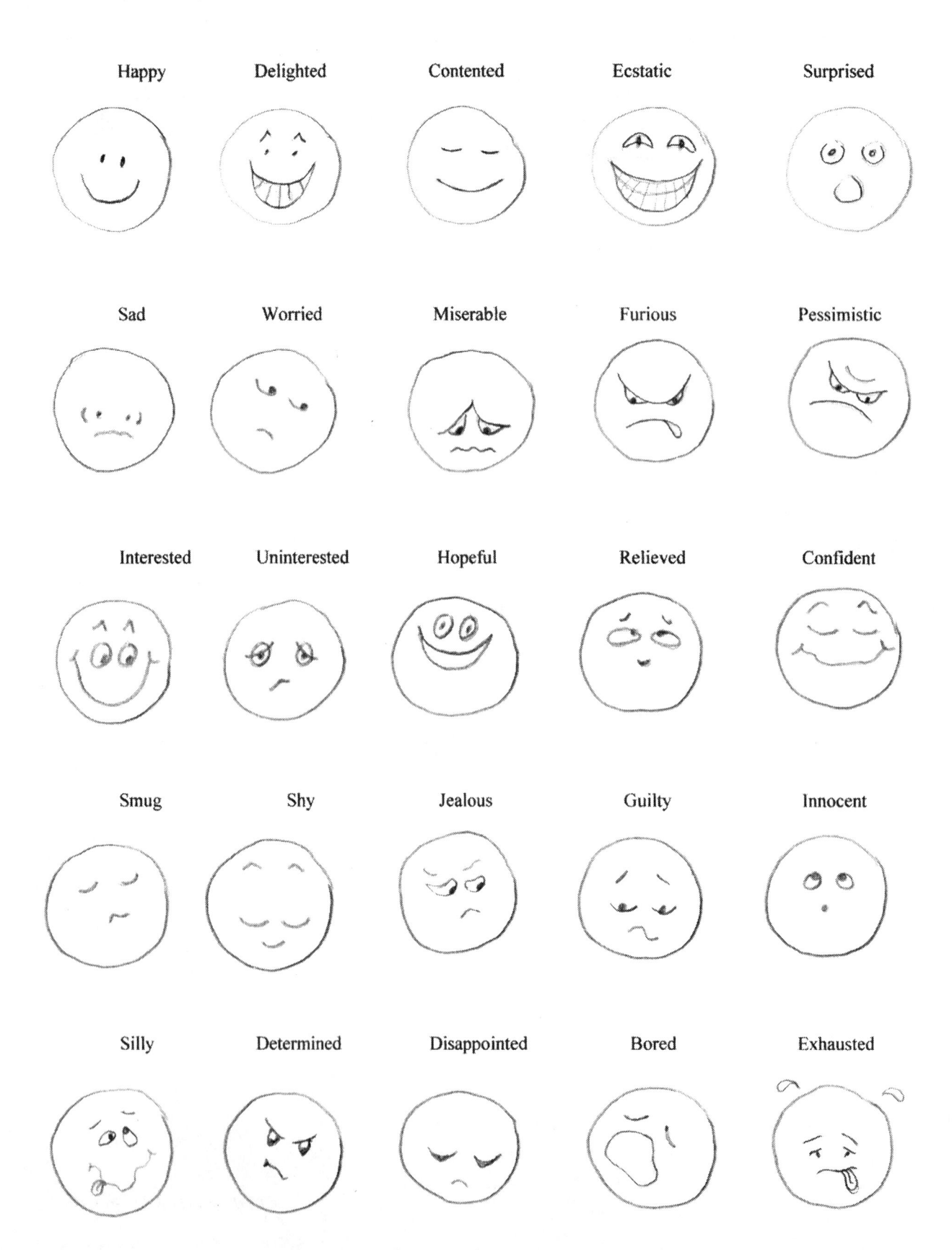

Happy	Delighted	Contented	Ecstatic	Surprised

Sad	Worried	Miserable	Furious	Pessimistic

Interested	Uninterested	Hopeful	Relieved	Confident

Smug	Shy	Jealous	Guilty	Innocent

Silly	Determined	Disappointed	Bored	Exhausted

To accompany the faces, there are some basic body movements. Move an arm or a leg here and there, and you can get just about any profile you need.

Here are some basic body movements that can be slightly altered for almost any position. Most figures work best if we draw the bodies first, and then add some clothes.

Standing   Walking   Running   Crawling

Notice that the walking guy gets his arms moving, and his knees have more angle than standing. The arms and legs of running are 90 degree angles. If you stand the crawling image straight up and make one back leg straight out, he could be climbing.

In the next group notice palms are facing up in giving, and palms are down in bending. Carrying big just means we do not have to show all of his arms in the picture, and in carrying small, we do.

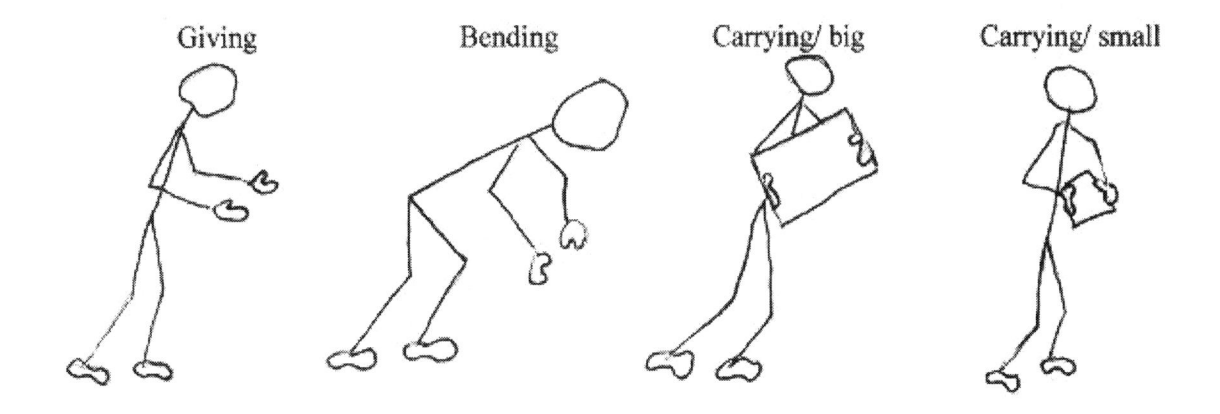

Giving   Bending   Carrying/ big   Carrying/ small

For dancing, he's just a big curve with palms up. Pulling and pushing are simply placing the arms in different positions. Sitting can be sitting at a desk, driving a jeep, eating at a table; it doesn't matter. This sitting position works for all sitting needs.

       Dancing   Pulling   Pushing   Sitting

The following figures represent a more complicated matter. Sometimes, in our letters we want to deliver powerful emotions, and those illustrations are a little harder to draw if we are not a good artist, such as Curly Grandma. The conclusion I finally came to was that emotions need hips and shoulders!

    Stickmen do not have shoulders and hips—clothes do. Emotional movement needs an anchor for the limbs. Drawing the clothes first and then attaching limbs help deliver that attitude or feeling. Look how simple the clothes are for hands on hips. Draw the clothes, add the limbs, and then draw the facial expressions.

    Hands on hip   Praying   Peek-a-Boo   Hugging

Remember, the more we do something, the better we get at it. The same applies in illustrating our letters. And, we don't even have to get good at this! Primitive drawings are perfect for what we are doing.

Besides being entertaining, illustrations deliver information, and in long letters they separate the text so the child can take a break and enjoy the letter. So, use lots of illustrations. They are important!

To aid us in our illustrations, I can recommend a couple of tools. They are not necessary, but if you are no good at drawing, these could assist you. They helped me immensely. The first thing I did was buy a child's art book. There are many inexpensive ones on the market. I bought a book by Ed Emberley. He shows you how to draw the simplest facial expressions, body movements, and even body types. You would be surprised how much you can do with one of his books.

The other tool I secured was a movable, wooden figure, which can be purchased at an art store or even one of those educational stores in the mall. I had trouble imagining what a body would look like in different positions, and this little model has movable joints, which can be maneuvered into all kinds of positions. This allowed me to visualize my figure and then put it onto paper. Besides, it looks cool sitting on my desk.

Do not forget to decorate the envelope. You can use stickers, stamps, or just about anything that adds color or "pop" to the envelope. This adds instant excitement to the moment the child receives the mail. To make sure you do not cause mailing problems by excessively decorating, you should check out Chapter 8: The Envelope.

The good thing about getting letters from kids is that they will always add illustrations!

The following letter is to Megan when she was about ten years old. It is a good example of using illustrations and comments to enhance the text. Florescent colors were used for the clothes and even the shoes. My granddaughter loved these illustrations and studied them for a long time. She counted the toothbrushes. She counted the girls and tried to remember each of these aunts as they are today, all in their 30s and 40s, with children. She even commented about the child standing too close to the stove.

Although this bug stationery is one of my favorites, if I were to write this letter today, I would use plain white paper because of all the detailed drawings. On this busy stationery illustrations fade away into the background.

Unfortunately, this letter is also a good example of some questionable grammar and punctuation. We can really be thankful for the illustrations—that is the only thing that produced new paragraphs! Sometimes, we just get carried away with telling the story and we forget all about the audience, as is the case in this letter. Still, we must keep in mind that corresponding is key, regardless of grammatical or mechanical flaws.

Letter to ten-year-old Megan:

Dearest Beloved,

I so enjoyed your letter and pictures. Thank you for writing to me. Reading your letter feels as though I am sitting down beside you as you are telling me all about Beauty. Your letter is just like a happy little visit. I love it! By the way, thank you for wishing me well on my home. You know, Megan, renting from someone is a whole new experience for me. As you may remember, renting means I am paying someone to let me live in their house while I look for another house that I can buy. I have lived in my own home for 28 years and I just can't seem to adjust to roaming about in a house that isn't mine.

I am trying to take especially good care of Mr. Kane's house. I try to keep all papers off the floor. I take my shoes off before I come into the house. I polish all the faucets so they shine like silver. I make my bed every single morning in case he has to come in for some reason. I always hang up my clothing. Every now and then I feel as though I am a child again trying to make my mother happy. Oh my, this does remind me of something that happened when I was about 12 years old. I think I shall tell you another tale of my rather interesting childhood.

One very <u>hot</u> Saturday, and it was oh so <u>very hot</u>. It was in the summertime and we lived in a very little house with a tin roof and no insulation! *(Insulation is stuff builders pack inside of walls and ceilings to keep the house cool in the summer and warm in the winter. A tin roof is something like putting a great big sheet of tin foil over the roof of the house, only thicker.)* So this house of ours was hot, hot, hot! Sometimes, I felt as though I lived in a popcorn popper! Well, not only was this house very hot, it was very tiny. Our whole house could fit inside just your living room, dining room, kitchen and breakfast room. Yes, my Dear, it was oh so very tiny. Just imagine that there was a Mommy, a Daddy, 9 girls and 2 boys all living inside this very hot, very tiny, little house. *(Who do you think might have been the oldest of all those 9 girls? Yes, it was your Curly Grandma.)* So, it was very, very difficult to keep this hot, little house clean. And do you know we had only 1 bathroom for everyone to share. Just 1 very tiny, little bathroom. That made it even more difficult to keep the bathroom clean. That bathroom was always a mess!

Now then, on this very hot day, I was a very busy 12-year-old girl, helping my mother. *(Do you remember who my mother is?)* As I watched her washing clothes, scrubbing the kitchen, and sweating and sweating profusely, I felt so very sorry for her. I wanted to do something extra nice for her. I wanted to do some very **deep** and very **thorough** cleaning for her. So, into the bathroom I went. I scoured the tub, the sink, and even the toilet. I scrubbed the floor and I even scrubbed the walls. Noticing the medicine cabinet was spotty; I began to clean every little fingerprint. It was then that I noticed all of our toothbrushes in a mangled pile inside the cabinet. It occurred to me that these toothbrushes were probably full of germs and they should not only be cleaned, but also sterilized! *(Did you know that sterilizing something means you must kill all of the germs by heating it up very hot?)* You see, Beloved, back in those days we had no microwaves or any contraptions to sterilize toothbrushes. So the only way to sterilize them was to boil them in a pot of water on top of the stove. And that is just what I did. A little pot just wouldn't be right for this job. Oh no, I retrieved the biggest pot in the kitchen, I don't know why, I just did. And I boiled all those toothbrushes for a very long time. While the 13 toothbrushes boiled, I happily sweated away, cleaning and cleaning. That very big pot of boiling water just heated up the very tiny kitchen and filled the entire back of the house with hot, hot steam. Our little house got hotter and hotter. Finally, my mother came to see what all the steam was about.

"GIRLS!" She yelled this at the top of her lungs as she lifted the lid of the boiling pot and she peered down into the cloud of steam. "GIRLS! WHO DID THIS? WHAT IS THIS? WHAT IS GOING ON?" As you probably figured out, I stepped up proudly to claim the glory of the extra labor (labor is work). It was a funny thing that my mother wasn't smiling.

Several of my sisters gathered around curiously, wondering about my mother's uproar as she stood there with a lid in her hand, sort of waving it around like a flag. I stood up on my toes, peered down into the steaming pot, which by now seemed to have an identity all its own, and swallowed my heart. There were no toothbrushes in that pot! There was a giant melted wad of plastic laying at the bottom of the pot! And floating all over the top of the water were millions, and I do mean millions *(or so it seemed)*, there were millions of little white hairy things floating all over the top of the boiling, steamy water. Yes, those little white things were the bristles of 13 toothbrushes. I had just ruined all the toothbrushes of the entire family!

Some help I was!

Considering what I had just done to our family's dental program, you would have thought my mother would have been very angry with me. But no, she let me explain, through my tears and sobbing, how I was trying to help her, how I was trying to do some very good, very deep and very thorough cleaning for her. I was so struck with her kindness, her smile and her hugs. She assured me it wasn't the end of the world, that our family would survive this catastrophe (even though we would have to wait until Dad's next payday to replace the toothbrushes). I knew then that I would always want to please my mother, that I would always want to be a help to her, not a problem for her. I knew then just how much I loved her for her kindness and understanding. I knew that I had the best mother in the world and I knew I was the luckiest kid in the world. And I knew that if I ever had any children, I would try to help them laugh at their mistakes and help them to know that everyone makes mistakes and mistakes will never be the end of the world.

Did you know LADYBUGS ARE GOOD BUGS?

And so my Beloved Megan, if you should ever happen to make a terrible mistake that makes you feel as though you want to crawl away into a little hole, just remember that you aren't making the first mistake. You aren't even making the biggest mistake. I, and all the other grandmothers in the world, and even all the other mommies and daddies in the world have made so very many mistakes before you. Everyone in the world makes mistakes. Mistakes are just a part of life. We will always be making mistakes. We just want to be sure to get over it!

OOPS   OH!   MY MY   OOPS

Just Get Over it!

Well, I hope you won't have to make too many mistakes in school, but if you do, remember to just get over it because everyone makes mistakes. I hope you have lots of fun in school. I hope you don't have too much homework because that ruins the day sometimes. I hope you like your teacher. I hope *she* doesn't make too many mistakes. And I hope every day is a wonderful day for you.

I shall write to you again, very soon I hope.

Goodbye for now,

Love and thinking of you always,

XXXOOO

Curly Grandma

Maybe one day I can see you at Lewis Elementary!

> Every child is an artist.
> The problem is how to remain an artist once he grows up.
>
> Pablo Picasso
> Spanish Cubist painter (1881–1973)

Rule #3: *Make it free.*

Do not expect a return letter. Sorrow and regret is sure to knock on your door if you hold a child to callous expectations and turn your correspondence into a scorecard. Disappointment will be yours because most children do not have an adult's sense of responsibility or propriety. Of course you are doing everything possible to encourage return letters. You are practically setting them up so they have to return a letter. But, you should write because you want to write a letter—not because you want to get a letter.

It is fair for grandparents to expect a letter more than rarely. And let us hope Mom or Dad is teaching the etiquette of letter return. We can help the parents coach the child about looking out for other people's feelings, and hopefully the child will understand how disappointed we will be if he does not return our letters. But, that is the most that can be done.

The grandparent will write many more letters than the child. That is because we grandparents are not strapped with hours of homework, (not to mention the soccer practice) and because we are the mature one in this relationship. Although school activities pile up, somewhere around nine years old, children are old enough to be prodded and reminded often about the reciprocating responsibility of letter exchange. Parents should tenderly insist their children 10 years and older sit down and write return letters, even if only a note; there are so many wonderful note cards available in stores now. But, even the most dedicated parent can not force a child to write letters from the heart.

So, fine-tune your influential skills and even dangle carrots if that is what it takes. Just remember, it is our job to write letters that grandchildren will anticipate, and our letters should inspire them to write back.

> Please write again soon. Though my own life is
> filled with activity, letters encourage momentary
> escape into others lives and I come back to my
> own with greater contentment.
>
> Elizabeth Forsythe Hailey (1938—)
> 'A woman of Independent Means'

Chapter 4

The Four E's

When writing to your grandchildren, keep in mind The Four E's: Easy, Entertaining, Engaging, and Everlasting. Each of these elements plays an integral part in a letter. We can better understand The Four E's by means of excerpts from sample letters.

Before we look at these samples, it is only fair to warn you that while writing to her grandchildren, Curly Grandma str-e-t-c-h-e-s grammar, punctuation, and usage rules. Hence, the examples in this chapter may avoid the label of certified grammatical crimes, but they probably qualify as probationary offenses. I am quite sure that there are many teachers and editors out there who wince and grimace at my ideas and recommendations. But, I think it is fun to explore and play with many types of style and punctuation with young children. I also think if a child has been exposed to new concepts before the technique is taught in school, it is not quite so foreign upon instruction, and then the child can better accept and understand the conventional usage in class. I do not think a little playing around with punctuation is going to damage my grandchildren by ruining their chances of finding good spouses or competing in the Olympics.

The hardest part about applying the Four E's is understanding that trying to do it keeps us from doing it. It is sort of like when you concentrate on not falling off a log, then surely, you will fall off the log. If we think we have to write wonderful, glorious drama or long, witty humor, then we hinder ourselves right from the beginning. This chapter will put us at ease by giving us a few little tricks that help our letters move from boring to appealing. It even reminds us of techniques we may already know, but have forgotten.

In The Four E's: Easy means simple, but employs profound understanding for our reader. Entertaining is interesting, but with summoned attention or perhaps with an exclamation point! Engaging is also interesting, but with attraction and invitation; possibly, we could even find our way to compelling. And, Everlasting is the element of writing with purpose: We want our letters to be here after we are gone as a window into our character and personality, so we write with that in mind.

The Four E's play upon each other. They should kindle each other, invite each other, and all should be present in each letter. Implementing The Four E's into our letters is what this chapter is all about.

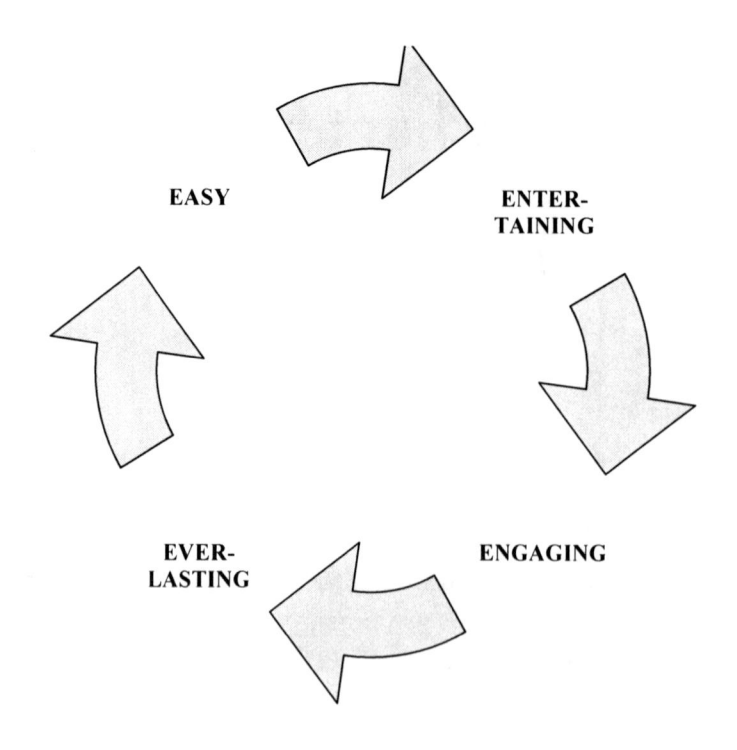

EASY → ENTER-TAINING → ENGAGING → EVER-LASTING → (back to EASY)

1. *Easy*

If we want to write letters that our grandchildren can read without assistance, we have to make them easy enough to read. This means we have to use their "learned" vocabulary if they are in or below second grade. This is a problem only for children younger than eight years old. Although their oral vocabulary is vast, young children between five and seven years old have a limited vocabulary that they have mastered in school for reading and writing. These learned words are the words that they can read and write independently. We tend to think of these "learned" words as short, three or four letter words, and that is partly true. However, most of their learned vocabulary consists of 220 words commonly known as the Dolch list. These words aren't necessarily decodable through phonics, and so they are also known as sight words. You would find words such as about and could in this list.

Let's not forget that we can always write letters to a young child that can be read aloud to him. And if that is our goal, it does not matter how difficult the vocabulary is because the child will be hearing the letter, not reading it.

It would seem that if we write with words that are not on this list then the child would not be able to read the letter. Yes and no.

Yes, our letters should be easy for the child to read and understand, but no, this does not mean we have to use only first-grade words for a first grader. On the contrary: We can use the grandest of vocabulary. Think about the old Mother Goose rhymes and fairytales. They hardly use primary vocabulary. We will sometimes find a high school readability level in these writings, but what they do use is an excellent way of explaining with lots and lots of details, or perhaps they use a literary trick such as repetition. Sometimes we will even find in these rhymes or tales, blatant definitions, or best of all, illustrations for clarity.

These are the same kinds of techniques we should employ in our letter writing. Our letters can consist of easy words and words that extend beyond the child's reading level; the language just has to be customized with some "trimmings" for comprehension.

Here are a few examples of techniques that can clarify new or challenging vocabulary for a child and consequently make it easy to read. The examples begin with excerpts fitting a five-year-old first grader and progress to an eight-year-old third grader.

Example:

We had fun.

We had fun with the Narnia DVD.

We had fun eating pop corn.

Techniques Used:

1. Repeating the words, "We had fun" on each line sets the child up to expect words that imply fun, and then he can probably figure the words out. Note there is only one sentence on each line.

2. Separating popcorn into two words turns a compound word into first grade words.

3. Instead of saying, "We had fun watching the Narnia movie" I used the word *with* and the word *DVD*; these are smaller words. DVD is culturally recognizable to children, and so the reader will be able to figure out the word, *Narnia*.

Example:

Sarah was livid! She was so very, very angry. Yes, she was livid!

Technique Used:

This line simply restates the meaning of livid in language the child can understand, and then repeats it.

Example:

I decided to sterilize the toothbrush (sterilize means to kill all the germs in the toothbrush).

Technique Used:

The definition of sterilize is placed in parentheses. Children love parentheses, and if you use them in *your* letters, you should not be surprised when your grandchildren's next return letter contains lots of parentheses. Do not worry if they use parenthesis incorrectly, it is natural that they experiment with new or unusual punctuation after observing it in your letters. One good side effect of letter writing is that correspondence becomes a safe and healthy environment in which grandchildren can practice grammar and punctuation without the fear of failing.

> Example:
>   Every morning I smelled the percolator—**that shiny coffee pot**— popping out a bubbly tune.
>
> *Technique Used:*
>   Putting the definition of the word inside dashes, parentheses, or brackets, and using different font, bold type, italics (anything that makes it jump out and be separate from the sentence) will help to explain the word.

Sum It Up: Easy

Some techniques we can use to make our letters easier to read:

- Use a controlled simple vocabulary, such as sight words, for most of the text
- Write one sentence on each line for five and six year olds.
- Use brief paragraphs and short sentences.
- Explain or define new or difficult vocabulary.
- Use dashes, parenthesis, brackets, or anything else that sets a word apart.
- Use different fonts or different size type for a definition.
- Repeat words or sentences.
- Give an example to explain new words.
- Give a specific definition for new vocabulary.
- Use the child's personal experiences for reference.

You can see that vocabulary in your letters can be challenging and new; it just needs to be clarified for understanding because the child will not be able to enjoy your letters fully if he or she is having a problem comprehending what is being stated.

For this reason you will also want to keep your paragraphs brief. It is better to break up your information into small chunks that the child can digest and the younger the child, the shorter the paragraphs should be. Use every trick available and supply lots and lots of details to get the message across to them. Remember what our teacher used to tell us? "Paint a picture with words."

2. Entertaining

For children, illustrations invite interest and provide explanation, clarification, and pure fun and entertainment. Any type of drawing, photos, stickers, or stamps will do the trick. In *Chapter 2: The Heart of Correspondence*, I explain how to "illustrate" with simple stickmen. Children love stickmen, and using these drawings will make your letters a sure winner.

Your letters should and will be entertaining if you write from the heart. Cues from the grandchild's previous letters will supply you with meaningful topics. Also, the tried and true, never failing to be interesting "olden-time" stories are good topics.

As you write, you should try to think of yourself standing at a campfire telling your story to the child. As you write, speak out loud along with your written words. Also, imagine your grandchild sitting next to you. Imagine her reaction, her response, and her questions and address these issues as you write. Now, your letter is entertaining the child.

Theatre is generally classified as drama or comedy. This can also be applied to your letters. Lay out a smorgasbord of emotions on paper. Letters can range from sad or poignant to amusing or riotous. Let's take a quick look at these opposing feelings.

Get Funny

Funny grips kids every time, but young children, around four to eight years old, may need extra help in the mental effort it takes to enjoy humor. If the child is laboring and concentrating on decoding the words, he tends to forget to enjoy the message. This is another reason why you will want to break up the information into brief paragraphs with short sentences.

Bending grammar, punctuation, and usage etiquette by adding some "ha, ha's" or doubling, or even tripling, exclamation points can sometimes be helpful. (Let the flogging begin, Editors!) It helps the child to know something funny is coming or happening.

The following letter to six-year-old Riley is an example of how a controlled vocabulary can still be used when trying to employ humor. Notice that I specifically point out to him that the incident of sitting on one of his toys is funny when I say, "This is like a funny joke." When he reads the letter, he can enjoy the humor and feel free to laugh at his Curly Grandma.

Letter to six-year-old Riley:

Hello My Biggie!

Did you know that I miss you?
I do.
I think about you a lot.

I think about you when I sit down.
Yes! When I sit down!

I sat down in my chair and HO!
I sat down on your Jack Sparrow man.

Ha Ha! You left him at my house.
You left him in my kitchen.
You left him in my chair!

And your Curly Grandma sat on Jack Sparrow.
He has a sword, too.
I sat on Jack Sparrow's sword!

This is like a funny joke.
A joke for your Curly Grandma.

Jack Sparrow's hair broke off.
I will glue his hair.
He will be fixed when you come.

Love,
And I think of you a lot,
When I sit down!

Curly Grandma

Use a Question

A question following a funny tidbit is also a good technique to ensure comprehension and an understanding of humor. Use all your tricks to help them grasp the idea that it was meant to be funny. These techniques will also work for setting up suspense. Take a look at this passage from a letter to an eight-year-old.

Curly Grandma's Letters · 63

There was no reason to be alarmed (upset) just because my mother had bought a gallon of catsup instead of a gallon of spaghetti sauce. What do you think will happen with that catsup? My mother was not about to let that very big pot of spaghetti noodles go to waste. No, No! My mother wasted nothing, not even catsup! She hurriedly (quickly) dumped that gallon can of catsup into the spaghetti. Yes, she did!

Oh, we were puzzled why that spaghetti tasted *unlike* her usual spaghetti. Ha ha! The joke was on us! Carmel thought...perhaps the meatballs were different. Ho! The joke was surely on us! Annette thought... perhaps we were all just unusually testy (cranky) on this hot day; that might account for this new mystery taste. Can you imagine what my mother was thinking while we were all sitting at the table?

But still, it *looked* like spaghetti...it *smelled* like spaghetti...and it was *in* the special spaghetti pot. At any rate, in a house with 11 children you don't wait to get a bite! You get your supper first, then ask questions. And that is just what we did. We ate the spaghetti made with catsup!!!! And then asked our mother why it tasted "funny".

Note the four explanation points: A definite No No in punctuation. It works for me!!

Melancholy:
Address the child by name

On another note, when you get melancholy or serious, you should address the child by name to pull them into your conversation. This helps to hold their attention and it sort of alarms them into concentration. Once in a while a sad or melancholy tone is fine, especially when the child has initiated that feeling in a previous letter, and we are responding to a sad subject. However, steer away from sad as much as possible. The following passage is an example of introducing a serious subject. It may help to know that when writing to my granddaughter, Megan, I always address her letters Dearest Beloved, and so Beloved is her name in this passage.

I will tell you a story about a Grandmother's very special experience. This story will relate to you just how the tiniest little things in life can affect one's heart and soul (if one is a sentimental old grandmother). You see, Beloved, you will find that you have been going through life, living your life, and just doing your everyday things, and Beloved, you have not even been aware that each of your little movements has been devotedly recorded on your grandmother's heart.

We letter-writing zealots can be too wordy. Unfortunately, I am proof. You will find many examples of "too wordy" in my letters. There is a fine line between using lots of details and becoming boring. Scout this out by reading the letter aloud. If it is long and "draggy" to you, it certainly is to the child.

Use visual contrast:
Use third person voice

    A good way to hold interest in a serious letter is to change fonts or size of print. Perhaps swing back and forth between them, being careful not to become distracting. Another grabber is to tell your story in the third person voice rather than first person, which is our natural tendency.

    Back to illustrating: drawing a solemn facial expression helps to serve up a dose of sobriety. Children are keenly aware of faces, and they assume the mood of the facial expression.

    The following is a melancholy letter utilizing the above strategies: calling out the child's name, changing fonts when adjusting mood or time, and using faces to deliver a mood. Megan was around seven years old when I wrote this letter to her, but she had always been an advanced reader and this letter was not too difficult for her. Besides, I knew her mother was only steps away just in case she tripped on a word.

Letter to seven-year-old Megan:

Dearest Beloved,

Hello! HELLO! I MISS YOU! **I DO SOOO MISS YOU!**
You have been in my thoughts almost as persistent as children at a mother's skirt! You seem to follow me throughout my daily routines. I suppose that is what happens to one who has moved away. I can only guess it's a type of buyer's remorse. Mommy can explain that to you better.

Now, I think I'll share a thought with you.
I will tell you a story about a Grandmother's very special experience. This story will relate to you just how important the tiniest little things in life can affect one's heart and soul, if one is a sentimental old grandmother. You see, Beloved, you will find that you have been going through life, living your life and just doing your everyday things and Beloved, you have not even been aware that each of your little movements has been devotedly recorded on your grandmother's heart.

Most stories begin with "Once Upon A Time", however this begins in a different manner, like this:

Sometime ago, approximately two and a half years ago, there was a little granddaughter who came over to visit me (I mean visit her grandmother)): She had a wonderful time. She played with some little toys that once belonged to her mommy. She played cards (I believe it might have been OLD MAID and GO FISH). She played some kind of checkers, or perhaps it was tic tac toe. She made cookies with her grandmother. She even enjoyed eating peanut butter and jelly and cereal for breakfast, lunch and supper. I believe she may even have gone grocery shopping with her grandmother beforehand, to pick out the cereal and the jelly. Then, evening fell. Well after a full day of playing she was certainly ready for a bath. So, as the grandmother drew the water, the granddaughter stepped into the tub.....

We must stop here for just a moment. You see, you must understand that this house of grandmother's was 28 years old. So many things in the house were very old. Most specifically, the tub was this old. Well, in order to keep such an old tub clean, one must scour it (*which means to scrub*). When one scours a tub, the tub becomes very porous, that means it will soak up anything that gets on it. So if you touch a freshly scoured tub with mud or grease the mud or grease will soak into it and stain it. Now, we can return to our story.

Now the granddaughter's feet were quite greasy and dirty from running around barefoot all day long, because as you know grandmothers don't make granddaughters wear shoes if they don't want to. As the granddaughter stepped into the tub, her little 4 year old foot left the most perfect footprint in the tub. The print of the toes was perfect. The print was a perfect picture of a perfect foot. The granddaughter didn't even notice the footprint. But the grandmother saw the footprint at that very moment. It was as if she felt the footprint press right down on her own heart. You would think she would clean it up immediately.

But, no, she fell in love with that silly little footprint and secretly she hoped it would never go away even after a good cleaning. Do you know that it never went away, even after 100 cleanings!

Very often, the grandmother would look into that tub and remember that wonderful visit from her granddaughter. That footprint looked just like a footprint to everybody else, but it was a reminder of a very special day for the grandmother.

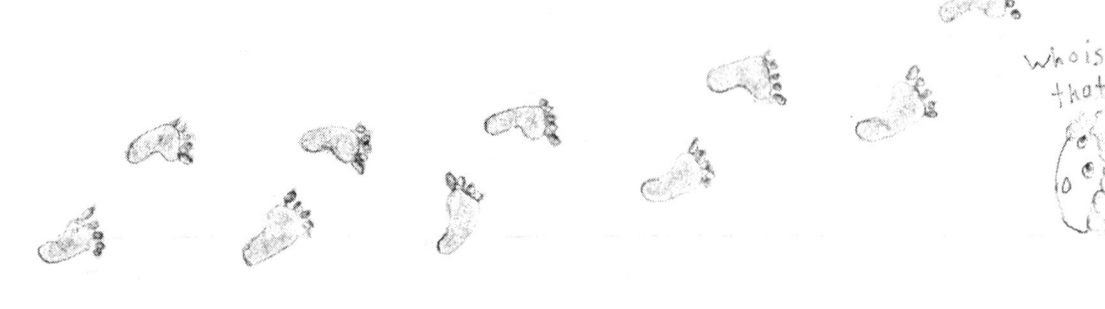

Well, after a few more years it was time for the grandmother to sell her house. She cleaned the house from top to bottom, spotlessly. And she even cleaned the tub. But still, the footprint stubbornly remained. When the house was sold and the grandmother drove away from her house for the last time, there was only one very special thing she could not take with her. She could not take her granddaughter's footprint with her and that made her so very sad. As she was driving away, a tear fell on her cheeks. But feeling sad was not something this grandmother liked. So, she had an idea. She went through all her pictures of her granddaughter and she found a shirt that she was wearing on the day the granddaughter was born. And do you know that shirt had a newborn footprint of the granddaughter when she was just born. It even had a date on it. It was 4-24-94.

Well Beloved, as I was saying at the beginning of this letter, we may not know it but even the smallest of things we do will leave footprints on someone's heart. So, let's continue to tread lightly throughout our life and leave the softest of footprints wherever we shall go. For surely, someone, somewhere, will feel each step.

Well, I must go now and begin working on my laundry. For it doesn't go away no matter how much I ignore it. I shall write again soon when my laundry is done and my belly is full of peanut butter sandwiches and I have had many days to catch up on *STUFF*.

I love you,

Curly Grandma

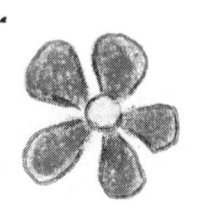

Babbling and rambling

It is a funny thing how babbling in verbal conversation is annoying, but in a letter it can be comical or entertaining—or at least different. When we stare at an empty sheet of paper and cannot write a single word, babbling works great—just when we think there is absolutely no way that we can be entertaining! The following letter was written to twelve-year-old Megan, a preteen who loves silly and different kinds of stuff. When it comes to writing, this age enjoys teetering on the edge of absurd.

This letter is not a shining example of good writing, because it comes right off the top of the head; it has no planning, no direction, no concern or respect for language or grammar and it most certainly is not even anchored in reality (just like babbling); it is good only on the level of entertaining a twelve-year-old. It worked for Megan. Nevertheless, it is an example of what can be written when there is nothing to write about. All it takes is … beginning.

Dearest Beloved, 9-1-06 (the longest day of my life)

It seems like a very long time since last I saw you. My goodness, how it seems so long ago that I saw you. How old were you then? Are you married yet?
I surely do wish I had something great to tell you. I so wish that I weren't always work—work—working. I tell you it is a lonely hard job... this writing stuff.
You can't imagine how it is to be typing on my computer. It goes something like this:
I sit at the computer and stare into the screen.
I move around to make sure my posture is pretty good.
I place my fingers over the correct keys.
I take my fingers off of the keys because my neck hurts.
I rub my neck.
I place my fingers over the correct keys.
I take my fingers off of the keys so I can scoot my chair up a little, not too much, though.
I place my fingers over the correct keys.
I stare into the monitor.
I look around the room.
I look at the keys.
I take my fingers off of the keys so I can scoot my chair back a little, not too much though.
I place my fingers over the correct keys.
I stare into the monitor.
I look at my printer, my mouse (I love this mouse. I wish it were a real mouse, HEY! I wish my monitor were a real Moniter lizard!), but... probably... they're not.
I look at my pencils.
I sharpen one pencil.
I test it.
I sharpen it again.
My pencil breaks. I wish my real mouse were here to chew on my pencils. That would keep them sharp, and then I wouldn't have to spend so much time sharpening them.
I sharpen another pencil.
I test it.
It breaks.
I sharpen it again. I can't believe how much I have sharpened today.
I wish my Moniter Lizard would chew my pencils nice and sharp for me so I wouldn't have to spend so much time sharpening them. Gosh, it's not like I have nothing to do!
I place my fingers over the correct keys.
I stare into my monitor, not the Moniter Lizard. He's goofing off, as always. I can't get that guy to show up. Just sharpen my pencils. That's all I ask. But NOOO. He has to go off and eat small mammals. He has to go out and bask in the sun. That lazy, good for nothing lizard! He may as well be a Geico, or gecko, or whatever that lazy thing on TV is.
I type... I.
I take my fingers off the keys because my neck hurts. Nobody knows how hard this job is. Nobody even cares. I just sit at this darned typewriter all day long, slaving over these letters, and NOBODY, NOBODY even notices.
I place my fingers over the correct keys.
I delete... I.

Well, grandparents, you get the point. You can see how babbling might work for you. No reason to finish the letter.

Sum It Up: Entertaining

Some techniques for making letters entertaining:

- Write from the heart.
- Illustrate!
- Draw facial expressions to deliver emotion.
- Be funny. Be silly. Babble.
- Include jokes, riddles, or pieces of literature.
- Use an explanatory! or a HA HA.
- Use questions.
- Address the child by name.
- Use visual strategies, such as changing fonts or print size or color.
- Use third person voice.
- Write about subjects in which the child is interested.
- Use computer-generated expressions.
- Illustrate and use stickers, stamps, or anything with color and POP!
- Choose stationery that intrigues or pleases the reader.

3. Engaging

The dictionary defines engaging as attractive or charming. An engaging letter is a letter that holds the child's attention, and it could actually be the same as interesting, except maybe a little more on the side of captivating. It engages the brain into the activity of imagination and participation. It is a letter that sticks with the child emotionally. It is taking interesting to the next step. Emotional feedback is the payoff for writing an engaging letter.

We want the child engrossed in the letter. One of the best techniques to accomplish this is to pay close attention to the language that is at work. You should let your words flow as if you are talking to the child, and you should try to use vocabulary that captivates the reader. Simply going to the thesaurus for meatier, more descriptive words can make a dull paragraph come alive.

The letter should have a setting, characters, and plot if possible. In other words, write your letter as if it were a story rather than a letter. Not all letters can use this application, but when possible, the letter is more fun and entertaining for both the writer and the reader when it becomes a story. You want the letter to emotionally pull the child into it, and yes, that is easier said than done, (Remember, do as I say, not as I do). It can happen with lots of practice: That is … write lots of letters and get good at it. Furthering the use of language as a lure will be discussed and explained in *Chapter 5: Hodgepodge and Mishmash*.

There are three essentials to an engaging letter:

1. Use the child's own experiences to compare or contrast your content.

2. Use illustrations to burn the message into the child's memory.

3. Use the main elements of a story: a beginning, middle, and an ending.

You can see a story format appearing in the next letter. The true star of the show seems to be the tuna shoe. But, it is a story about poverty and not being able to afford new shoes. It is a story of embarrassment, but told in a cheerful and humorous nature. It uses story language such as, "… those shoes had to walk to and from school each day," and, "And so it was that we lived half of the year with…" This type of language makes the child think that she is reading a story out of a storybook. We can also see how it draws on Hannah's experiences. It uses her behavior of not wearing shoes (about which her whole family teases her) as the foundation of the letter.

If we can forgive how many paragraphs start with "well," and if we can ignore perilous punctuation, it qualifies as fun and engaging.

Letter to nine-year-old Hannah:

My Sweetie, My Sweetie,

How have you been? I have been thinking of you more than often. Well, to be honest, I think of you each and every day.

Today, as I was putting on my shoes to go to the store, I thought, "I wonder if Hannah is wearing shoes today. I wonder if she is running about the fields in shoes, or in her tough little bear feet—muddy between the toes, crusty on the soles, and yet tender enough to snag a splinter or thorn. I wonder how Hannah's feet are doing today." Yes, My Sweetie, I often think of your little feet and all the rest of you, too.

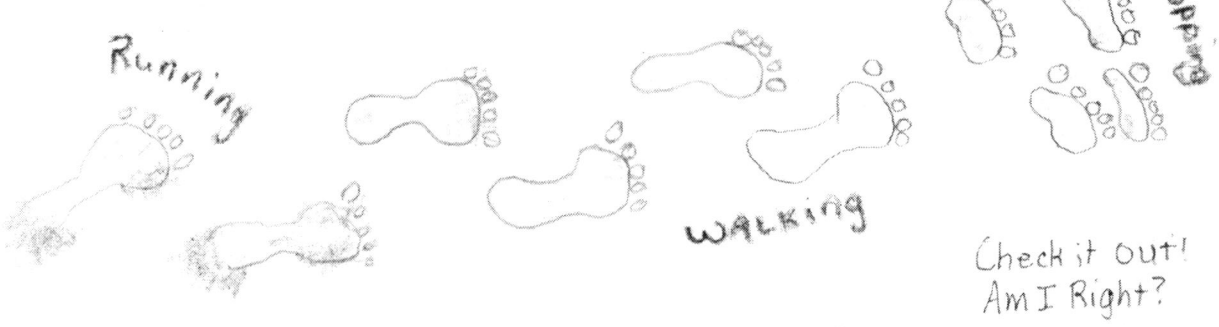

Running *Walking* *Hopping*

Check it Out! Am I Right?

As I was thinking about your feet, I began to think about how I used to run around barefoot, as a child. You, Hannah, You don't wear shoes because you love the feel of the earth beneath your feet; because you are your mother's wonderful wild child. You need to be part of the earth when you explore and experience all the luscious senses of the earth. I, on the other hand, didn't wear shoes because my shoes had holes in them.

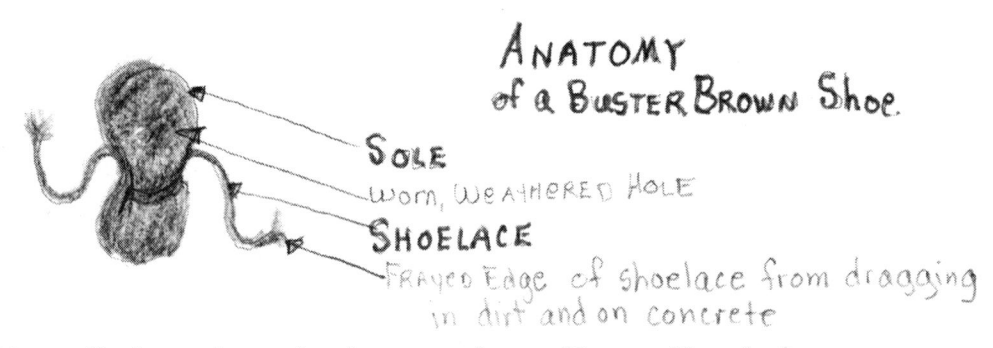

Anatomy of a Buster Brown Shoe.
Sole — Worn, Weathered Hole
Shoelace — Frayed Edge of shoelace from dragging in dirt and on concrete

We could not afford new shoes when I was growing up. You see, Hannah, there were no Walmarts or discount stores when I was a child. Did you know that a new pair of shoes cost around 20 or 30 dollars back then? Did you know that when I was sixteen-years-old, I would work for a whole week to get $30.00? One Christmas, my sisters and brother pulled all our money together to get our mother a new pair of black patent leather shoes. The cost was about $40.00.

Well, anyway, back to my original point. When I was very young, about five-years-old, my mother certainly couldn't afford new shoes for us. Remember, my father was dead and my mother was raising John, me, Sarah, Danielle and Kathy all by herself. We were living in Keemom and Keebob's house at 1053 E. Rose St. in Lakeland. Remember that

Keemom and Keebob are my mother's parents. They are really John and Carmel Sandella, but we called them Keemom and Keebob.

Well, Keemom and Keebob lived in two houses. They lived in a house up North in Ashtabula, Ohio from Easter until Halloween because it was cooler up there in the summer time. Then when it was about Halloween time, they would come down to the little bungalow house on Rose St. And they would spend the winter in Florida with us. It's funny how I always thought that they were coming down to live with us when, in fact, we were actually living with them. Poor Keebob had tuberculosis, a breathing disease, and so he could not handle the cold snowy winters in Ohio.

And so it was that we lived half of the year with Keemom and Keebob. They were what one might have called misers in the old days. That would be penny pinchers, or in a much nicer tone, today—savers. They were actually cheap, frugal magpies. And squirreling away every available bit of money, food, clothing and even shoes was a must in our family. We never threw anything away because it could be "recycled" into something else. Recycling of this nature was Keebob's favorite hobby.

That brings me back to shoes. Even though shoes did cost more back then, they were not necessarily made better. They still wore out pretty darned fast. And if these shoes had to walk to and from school each day, they wore out much faster than expected. My Buster Browns seldom lasted more than a couple of months. Not to fear, though: Keebob was always rescuing my shoes.

I remember many mornings eating my cereal at the little round table with the red-checkered tablecloth while Keebob worked on my Buster Browns. He would fix the big round hole in the sole of my shoe in this way:
- Open a can of tuna or soup.
- Take the top part of the can that comes off when you open it—we called it a lid, but it's really just the top.
- File down and sand down all the rough cutting edges of the lid so it's not sharp.
- Lay my holey part of the shoe on the lid and trace the shoe outline on the lid.
- Cut the lid so it will fit inside the shoe.
- File down and sand away all the sharp edges one more time.
- Place the form-fitting tuna lid inside the shoe and *VOILA*, it's a new sole.

Yes, this new tinny sole gave my Buster Browns a much longer life. It was fine for walking and running at home, and well, you know, just everyday stuff. But, it was quite embarrassing on the playground at school. When I was on the swing, all the kids could see the bottom of my shoe and they would ask, "What's wrong with your shoe?" And when we walked in line, the guy behind me would hear the click, ….., click, ….., click, …… It was sort of like having taps on your shoes, but just on one shoe. And usually my sock would get hung up on the piece of tin and get torn or get dragged down off the back of my heel and pulled up into my shoe. Then I spent the rest of the day constantly saying, "Wait, I have to pull up my sock."

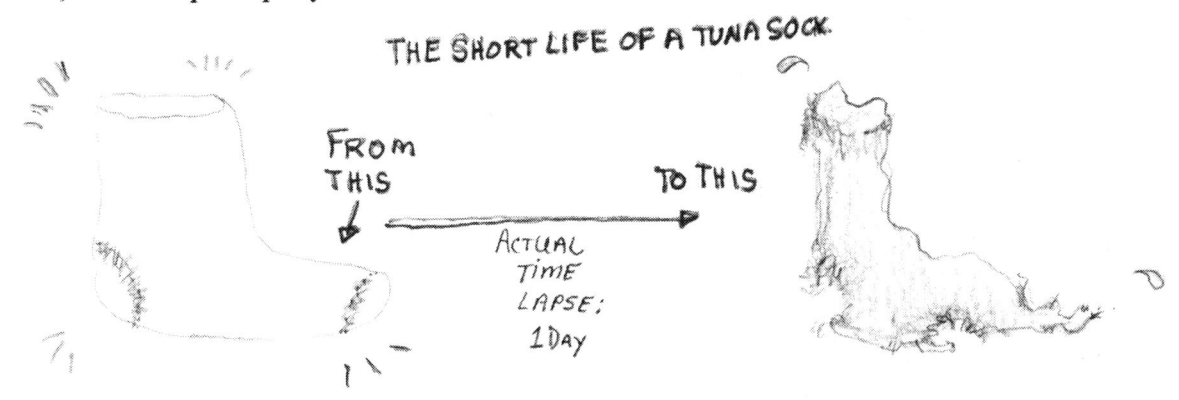

THE SHORT LIFE OF A TUNA SOCK.

FROM THIS → TO THIS

ACTUAL TIME LAPSE: 1 DAY

All this worked great for my shoe's long life, but unfortunately, my flimsy socks wore out so quickly that I had to resort to wearing Keebob's socks. They, of course, were too long, so I had to fold them down under my feet when I slipped my feet into my shoe. And then, the socks were so thick in my shoe that my feet hurt all day. (It's a good thing that Keebob was a short little Italian guy). Too bad socks weren't cheap. We could have used a few extra pair for our "tuna shoes".

Well, it wasn't just me who wore tuna shoes. It was all of us kids. I don't remember Keemom or Keebob or even Mom wearing tuna shoes, but I guess I just didn't pay much attention to their shoes. I guess tuna shoes are the reason that I never wore shoes for play time around the house. The only time I ever wore shoes was when we went somewhere and Mom made us wear them. So, when I see that you never wear shoes, I am just jealous. I wish that I were still a kid running around with "diamonds on the soles of my shoes", or just plain barefoot.

Well, I must go now, for I have no diamonds, but I do have a can of tuna that is going to get opened in a few minutes. For, I have three boiled eggs that need to be used up quickly and tuna salad on toast with a lettuce leaf and a slice of tomato will be just the right thing for my insatiable appetite.

Then, I think I will look around for some old shoes.

Love, and thinking of you always,

xxx   Curly Grandma
ooo

Missing you with all my heart

Sum It Up: Engaging

Now, how do we write engaging letters? A recap tells us that children will mentally participate in our letters and retain the information of our written words when we:

- Illustrate!
- Write from the heart.
- Write with our own voice.
- Imagine that we are actually talking to the child when we write.
- Compare and contrast with the child's own experiences.
- Use humor and stimulating punctuation with humorous expressions (ha ha, short of overkill for very young children).
- Use sorrow sparingly.
- Use unexpected punctuation.
- Use parentheses, dashes, brackets, and ellipses...
- Use italics and bold and underlining.
- Use brief paragraphs.
- Write with lots of details and explanations (paint pictures with words).
- Use interesting language.
- Use familiar language.
- Use words that have a great rhythm.
- Use new vocabulary.
- Use familiar vocabulary.
- Clarify and explain new vocabulary.
- Address the child by name.
- Address a question to the child.
- Write in a different tense, or try third person instead of first person.
- Change fonts.
- Change size of print.
- Use a different color for important print.
- Break the rules!!!
- ENJOY!
- Did I say ILLUSTRATE?

As time passes, you will discover more engaging techniques, but these are enough to get you started on writing some great letters. Always, the best way to write an engaging letter is to write from the heart with your own voice: Tell what you want to say in print, but tell it as though you are talking.

Using these techniques assures that your grandchildren will mentally picture and record the letter's events and question you about the details when the opportunity arises. Remarkably, your grandchildren will even begin copying your style in their letters. Trust me; this is the grandest of compliments.

4. *Everlasting*

What do you want your grandchildren to know? How do you want to be remembered? What events and what people are important in your past? You are the only one with these answers. You have a lot of family information that only you can provide. Words in print are here to stay, so your correspondence will become a record of your life experiences. Your letters will become a resource for future generations. Write each letter with this in mind. But, what really matters is that you pick up that pen or sit at your computer and write! That way you officially become an inkslinger—blessed with an eager audience. Now, that's timeless!

Writing is easy. All you do is stare at a blank sheet of paper until drops of blood form on your forehead.

Gene Fowler, author of Skyline, Good Night, Sweet Prince: The Life and Times of John Barrymore (Lively Arts Series), and Minutes of the Last Meeting

Chapter 5
Hodgepodge and Mishmash

Children love literature. Mostly, they love folk tales. They twitch with tension when hearing about bread crumbs disappearing. They will spill out of their seats and ransack a living room like drunken sailors after becoming intoxicated with the majesty and power of St. George slaying a dragon. And then they once again become domesticated when their ears are pricked with "Once upon a time long, long ago, in a far away land." For this is the power of the language of folktales. Even the repetition and rhythm of Mother Goose captures their attention.

Myths, legends, fables, fairytales, and limericks: they are all folktales, and they are all peddlers of ritual phrases, elegant expression, elaborate repetition, and enchanting narratives that entice and capture a child's imagination. Across the world, children will beg for their favorite folktale to be read to them again and again because they never tire of it. They remember the tale almost word for word. Furthermore, they seem to love every type of adaptation. It is the language of folk tales such as "John Henry," "The Three Little Pigs," and "Rumpelstiltskin" that inspires children to seek out these stories and return to them repeatedly.

These tales usually have a melodic spirit with deep imagery. The rich language enchants and engulfs the child in a world of adventure and exploration. The tales themselves are of another time in imaginary worlds with certainty gone astray. Through these tales, young children are allowed to rehearse dangerous and precarious experiences; and so children are able to emotionally participate and try out the story's events.

Folk tales never leave us. They evolved, before writing, from centuries of storytelling for the purpose of explaining origins, infusing values, and passing on tradition and memorable events. All aspects of life were embedded in these tales, from daily life to exotic, romantic adventures. They emitted powerful human passion and left us with moral lessons fixed in the very fabric of our souls.

Although somewhere around our teen years we scoff and mock these tales, we always return to them and enjoy them. Whether we return through movies or theatre, or simply to share them with our own children, the folktale's allure renders us helpless, and again as adults we embrace them because of their simple wit, wisdom, charm, and characters.

Conjure a charm

It is the language of the folktale that attracts us, so why not use that genre as a tool in your letter writing? Your letters need not be tame, nor need they dutifully conform to the expected language of normal letters. Muck around and give rise to colorful, embroidered letters crafted in the company of wonder and marvel. Plunder through the language of hodgepodge and mishmash. As a writer you should never fear to steer your course to the epicurean "Once Upon A Time" or "Happily Ever After." Your letters are your legacy, so let your story be told in storybook language. Enchant your grandchildren with kindred tales and they will respond in a delightful fashion!

> Neither blatherskite, nor gasbag are we, Nay,
>
> Simply a man of letters, a penwoman, or wordsmith on a good day,
>
> With a story, a notion, a legacy for say.
>
> AB

It is because we have lived that we have a story to tell. Simple emotions and actions such as wanting and toiling give us validation. Our everyday achievements, as small as planting a seed or as large as building a corporate empire, are landmarks in our story. The breath of our child and the beat of our land give us deep sentiment that needs only to be pondered and placed on paper. Our love of wonder and our awareness of family, as a child and as an adult, have prepared us and will provide endless resources for our storytelling. Therefore it is time to apply pen to paper, embrace storybook language and authenticate our life.

The following letter was written to my granddaughter, Megan Leigh, my first grandchild, when she was around ten or eleven years old. She once told me that of all her letters from Curly Grandma, the following correspondence was her favorite. Could it be that it reads like a fairytale with folktale language? A sentence such as: "…it was almost too quiet when it happened" sets the child up for excitement, as does "Galloping toward us was an enchanting white spotted steed." Phrases such as "...we hiked deep into the woods..." and "Things would not work out so perfectly..." help to place the child in another world and another time, and it hints at suspense. It does not matter that I am not a great writer. Any time my letters dapple in storytelling charm, it will be a success with a child.

This letter has all the ingredients of a classic tale. It has characters entwined in a plot of struggle, and it ends with a happily-ever-after mood. It was a true event in my life. I just imagined telling a campfire story when putting it down on paper. And I told it like a fairytale. Most people could tell this story in a matter of a few sentences. I too, could have done so, but I recounted all of my emotions and detailed many of the small elements in the experience. Who knew it would be such a hit?

Because I was dog-tired when I wrote this letter, I chose not to illustrate. Instead, I used shiny foil letters in the margin to deliver messages. The messages carried the mood, the feelings, and the values that I wanted to convey to Megan. The messages include: lost and found, adventure; 1, 2, 3; bravery, courage, unselfish, and destination.

Letter to ten-and-a-half-year-old Megan:

LOST AND FOUND

Dearest Beloved,   1-24-02

How is my little Megan? It has been nearly three weeks since last I saw you. I miss you and think of you always. Three weeks is much too long. I shall have to make a new visiting rule that says: Never shall more than two weeks pass between visits. THERE! IT'S DONE! Now, if we can just conjure up some means of enforcing it, we'll be content. OH WELL! So much for my wizardry!

As you know, I am very busy building my new house. It feels very much like doing homework every day for eight hours a day. I never get to quit thinking about how the rooms will look or how the windows will fit, or even how big the hall will be. Each day has new demands that must be met. I'm doing my best to make it all fit perfectly. I can't wait for the day that you and Mommy and Daddy and Hannah can come to see it. I know that will be a long way off, but nonetheless, I keep looking forward to that day.

I am also staying very busy with babysitting your little cousin, Riley. When I hold him, it takes me back to a time when I used to hold you and Hannah when you were cuddly, little babies. There is something special about holding a baby. It feels like a piece of heaven has been loaned to me.

Well, I wonder what kind of new things have been going on in your life? I wonder if you've been on any adventures, lately? If you were a grandmother you wouldn't have many adventures, but I can tell you about one of my surprise adventures last Friday.

You see, Beloved, I have been so very busy with the house, that I needed to get away and have some quiet time. So that seemed best accomplished by getting out into the woods, strolling by the lovely rivers and listening to the turkey calls. That is just what we did. We drove far away to a beautiful forest, Jennings Forest it is called. As we drove

ADVENTURE

deep into the woods, I noticed a road sign that said Cemetery Road. I wondered what was down there, but said nothing. I sat in silence bumping along in the seat feeling every hole and every rock in the dirt roads. All this bumping felt quite relaxing and I enjoyed swaying and rocking in the truck as if I was in some heavenly place. I was ready for some quiet country time. We did take along our ultralite fishing rods, armed with beetle spins, just in case! And so we hiked deep into the woods to the fishing river.

Life was so quiet and almost too peaceful when it happened. You would never guess what emerged in front of us, yet across the river. Galloping toward us was a most enchanting white spotted steed, mounted by a beautiful young girl. She was wearing an English helmet and sat upon a very formal European saddle. Her stirrups seemed so very high and her saddle looked to be no more than a heavy blanket, yet it did have a horn. She sat upon that Arabian as though she grew up in the saddle. But you see, Beloved, she was on the other side of the river. So, we stood there holding our fishing rods staring at this stamping horse with the beautiful mistress. We were frozen in this moment.

"Where are we? Can you tell me how far it is to Middleburg?" From across the river, the girl fired questions with a thick accent. It took me a moment of concentration to understand what she had just asked. I was stunned to think this wasn't a dream. This was a real live girl on a real live horse and she seemed lost. Just about the time I returned to reality, another horse, mounted by a young blonde girl, and yet a third horse also mounted by a young girl pounded the ground and snorted and circled. All were across the river looking very alarmed and centered on making some kind of decision.

"How deep is this water, here? Can it be crossed? If we should cross, where should we be headed?" The first two girls continued firing questions at us faster than we could answer them. I could now see these girls were quite young and seemed highly concerned. It began to sink into my mind that the girls had probably been out riding for quite some time. Looking at my watch, I knew there was only about an hour of daylight left and I now understood their urgency. Yes indeed, they were lost and night was soon to be at our heels.

After exchanging a few more questions and answers, we arrived at these conclusions: Sarah was 16 years old, flawlessly commanding a white Arabian and she was from Spain. She spoke with a very strong accent. Now I understood the European saddle. Jennifer, the blonde 14 year old, rode a brown Arabian and she also seemed an excellent equestrian. Far away, still on the other side of the river with the other girls, but staying much farther away, was Tiffany, a little blonde, 13 years old, who was shy and not very good at riding horses. She seemed very upset and even her Arabian was stamping and circling. I decided the horse must sense Tiffany's apprehensions.

These girls were determined to make it across the river to get to us. They were afraid to continue on their path since dark was soon to be here. My friend had calculated that they had come 4 hours into the forest and it would be about 10:00 at night before they could make it out of the forest. We tried to help them figure out a way to make it out on their same path, but no. They knew they wanted to be with us because that way they would be safe. But how? They were on the other side of the river.

Well, you know, Beloved, if you are ever in a pickle and you know you have to be brave, here's what you must do: You must find some courage somewhere deep down inside of yourself, you must slow down, take a deep breath, and visualize (that means see a picture of yourself in your brain doing something very brave).

That is just what Sarah did. She stared out across the river in silence. She leaned down and whispered into Charisma's ear. She held her little crop tightly in her fist. Then, in a burst of thunderous courage, she veered her horse down the deep embankment and steered Charisma right into the water. It looked as if this action was going to be perfectly executed. But Charisma was afraid. She stamped into the water and it got so deep so quickly, that she turned and tripped and clamored back onto the dry bank. Sarah was relentless. She stared across the river, repeated the same whisper into Charisma's ear, and used her little crop to whip Charisma back into the water. "Heeyah!" "Heeyah!" She urged Charisma into the deep water. The water immediately rose up to the horse's neck and I was shivering to see this because that water was bitterly cold. Sarah held on tightly and then we realized Charisma wanted to turn around again because there was a fallen tree under the water. Charisma had to swim across it. She did. She did it beautifully. The horse and the girl exploded out of the water onto our side of the river. We cheered and smiled and slapped each other on the back as if we were baseball players who had just won a big game. We had just witnessed a very courageous act. At that time we began calling Sarah, "The Spaniard". We gave her that name after a hero in a movie. The hero was a general from Spain who rode a white horse and saved many lives in many battles of war. Sarah was indeed deserving of such a title.

Now that "The Spaniard" was safe on our side of the river, we began coaxing the other two girls to cross the river. We did so because we knew we could lead them out of the forest to our truck. Once there, we could call their parents to bring the horse trailer and pick them up. And so this plan seemed perfect. Jennifer began coaxing her horse into the water. The horse stamped and disagreed with her but finally trampled down the deep embankment and dove into the icy water. Although this pair didn't make it across as perfectly as "The Spaniard", they still did make it across and again we cheered like a baseball team.

Now for little Tiffany, with her long blonde hair and shy quiet little voice, things would not work out so perfectly. You see, Megan, the kind of courage we just witnessed is something that comes along when one becomes about 14, 15, or 16 years old. Tiffany wasn't about to charge down the steep embankment into that icy water and trip and get crushed under one thousand pounds of horse muscle. And so, hopelessly we all took turns trying to convince little Tiffany, who had tears streaming down her face, to cross over. The more we tried, the harder she cried. Finally, there was nothing to do but swim across the river to Tiffany and lead her horse back across the river to us. Well, Beloved, just how dark do you think it is getting, now? That's right. We were running out of daylight and we still needed to spend about a half-hour walking to the truck.

Sometimes, especially in real life and not as much as in fairy tales, the very person who seems to be not so adventurous, or not so brave, or even just not so special in any way, just seems to step up and do the most courageous thing. None of us wanted to go swimming in that icy water to go get Tiffany and her horse, but after much discussing, Jennifer looked at me and said, "Will you hold my horse? She doesn't like her reins tight, so hold them lightly". She then dismounted, and still fully dressed and booted, she swam across the river. She brought the horse across but Tiffany still refused to cross because the river was so deep and because she was carrying all the girls' possessions. My friend walked along and found a tree that had fallen across the river. The tree was lying across the river like a natural bridge and so Tiffany crossed over on the fallen tree to our side. Meanwhile, Jennifer was now shivering and looking quite blue. I was quietly admiring how she had taken on this uncomfortable task without complaining an thought that my own daughters would have accomplished such a deed.

Dark was closing in on us and we hurried down the path into the woods. We all made small talk and found out about each other as we raced against time. The girls stayed on their horses and as quickly as possible we made our way to the truck. Reaching our destination, we immediately called their parents and gave directions to our meeting place, which strangely turned out to be a hundred-year-old church and a graveyard.

This seemed a fitting place to end such an adventure. As I watched Jennifer shivering, I got a jacket out of the truck. She slipped it on with a slight smile and she said, "I hope my Mom won't be too mad. I probably have her very worried." I knew we had helped some very nice girls. They had made a very serious mistake by not paying attention to time. They were lost and then found. It was a good ending.

For me, this was a good adventure because I got to revisit a time when I was growing up with all my sisters. i remembered setting out on a "walk" with my sister, Danielle, and being lost for many hours. I remember thinking that my mother was home worrying about me. I even told that story to the girls as we trekked through the forest to the truck. I will always remember my adventure with Danielle and I will always remember Sarah, "<u>The Spaniard</u>", Jennifer, <u>the heroine</u> and Tiffany, <u>the young</u>.

You, Beloved, will experience many adventures in your life. I hope you will write them down in your "memory" and even in a journal and share them with your children and grandchildren one day.

So much for story telling. I shall have to go and pick out some tile for the house, so goodbye for now. I love you. I miss you. And I think of you always.

Love,
Curly Grandma

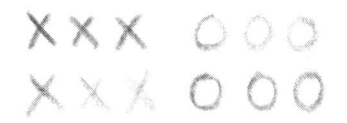

XXX OOO
XXX OOO

> They have been at a great feast of languages,
> and stolen the scraps.
>
> William Shakespeare, "Love's Labour's Lost", Act 5 scene 1
> English dramatist & poet (1564 - 1616)

Chapter 6

Target Your Audience

Read-Aloud Letters
Writing to Babies and Toddlers

Writing to our grandchild seems simple in that we know what information we want to share with them. It becomes more complex when we have to determine how to share that information. We need to think about the child's age and maturity level if we want the child to enjoy the letter independently. We have to target the child with language and style that the child can understand. There is no "one size fits all" for children's letters. We simply cannot write to a three-year-old the same way that we write to a nine-year-old.

There are many books that explain how children understand verbal and written language. We do not need an in-depth study, but it does help to know what and how children understand, if we are going to write to them. That's the goal of this chapter. I have included examples of both autobiographical and friendly correspondence to demonstrate how we target certain age groups. Our letters will usually be styled in one of two forms: as a letter to be read aloud to the child or as a letter to the child as an independent reader. Examples of both styles are presented in this chapter.

Read Aloud Letters
Birth to Three-Years-Old

Once you decide to write to your new grandchild, have a heartfelt conversation with the parents informing them that you want to begin this correspondence as your written legacy. Explain that your letters will become a family history to save as a gift for the child. It is important to let the parents know you are not expecting letters in return. Your only expectation is that the parents save the letters.

If you are lucky enough to have grandchildren whose parents read to them from the time they are born, then your letters will fit perfectly into this tradition. The length of the letter does not matter because its function at this time is to bond the parent and child to the letter-writing experience. You are just getting the parents accustomed to holding the child in their lap and reading your letters aloud. You can put in some illustrations and decorate with stickers and stamps so Mommy and Daddy, and even the child, one day, can get a good chuckle out of reading these family narratives.

Reading together and eating meals together rank as possibly the most bonding of all family traditions. Your letters also encourage and contribute to family unity. They may even become a favorite family custom.

You can begin writing letters to your grandchild from birth. You don't have to wait until the child is old enough to read. Give the letters to the parents to enjoy for the first year of the child's life. What parents wouldn't appreciate reading family history presented in a personal letter? Anybody can look at a family tree: lines with names connected to each other. But very few people have family trees presented with personality, voice, perspective, and emotional impact.

Your first letters to the newborn will welcome him into the family with stories of his birth. Then, start at any point on the family tree that feels comfortable to you. Your descendents will want to know you (the inner you) from what you can recall from the past. Tell your history the way you remember it, with warm stories, but interspersed with poignant specifics. Be sure that you address the child by name in each letter because you are building a gift for this grandchild, a very personal gift. Give the parents a notebook, and have them start saving your letters.

The goal is for you to be writing your family history in letters while you wait for the child to become old enough for true correspondence. If you are not comfortable with the idea of writing letters to a newborn, go ahead and write the letters, but do not mail them. Many people find it less intimidating and easier to write letters when they know they will not be mailed. Save all the letters in a notebook, and when the child is old enough to receive letters and show interest, or when you feel you are ready to involve the parents, then deliver the notebook. In the meantime, just be sure the notebook is clearly labeled so that if something happens to you, it will be given to the child.

Many professionals agree that we should start reading to children at infancy. This might sound silly, but babies enjoy listening to a parent read aloud to them. Infants love the sound of the voice and the rhythm and tempo of conversation. Your letters can be part of their read-aloud program.

If the parent would not read to a newborn, introduce the letters with a tape recording of your voice reading them aloud. After several months of receiving both letters and tapes, the parents will probably become comfortable with reading the letters to the child.

Usually, corresponding with a newborn is something that people embrace fully and lovingly or it is something that they see as foreign and absurd. There seems to be no middle ground here. You may like or dislike this correspondence based on how the parents feel about it. The parents' warm, supportive embrace or contrary, aloof position, may affect you. Understandably, a cool reception to your poured-out efforts could shackle your enthusiasm and passion.

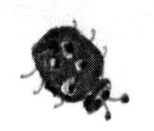

My Blessed Emily,

Me, So Proud! So Happy!

I have long awaited your arrival and must say my heart has been captured by your beauty and innocence. Much happiness flourishes in your Curly Grandma now that you are here. Welcome to the world, Blessed Emily, and welcome to your family.

It is with the warmest of kindred pride that I welcome you, my granddaughter. You are but an infant, yet I am compelled to share with you what luck it is that you have been born to such dear parents and sisters.

Better parents could not be found for you anywhere in this world. Your mommy and daddy are the noblest of parents. They do not hold silly and fashionable effects in esteem. They champion the good and they enable fine and decent values to flourish in the household. They are most capable of providing you with a lifetime of knowledge and affording you experience in manners necessary for a virtuous life.

Your mother is an endless reserve of affection, encouragement and guidance. Your father will be your defender and he is a chivalrous provider in all areas of need.

It is with great luck that you come to them.

My pride would also like to introduce you to your sisters. Never have I met young girls who are genuinely happy for others who fall upon good fortune. This is a most endearing quality for sisters to possess. For it is with your sisters that you will exercise both leisure and labor.

There is no doubt that Megan will escort you into the world of knowledge and sophistication. She is proficient in numbers, language, music and in all manners where you will need assistance.

It is certain that Hannah will one day lay the groundwork for the humanity necessary to respect our fellow beasts and pets of this world. She will pilot the principles for compassion and humility.

Your sisters are the blessings of good and loving parents and so they will bring you much joy. With you, they will burden your lowest of times and applaud your finest efforts. And they will be there for you. They will always be there for you.

Yes, Emily, it is with great luck that you come to them.

Blessed Emily, I know little of you now, but I know who you will become. You will join your family and become a kind and gracious beauty. You will master the art of consideration and thoughtfulness because you are born into it. You will inherit the love of mankind and grow with a compelling yearn to contribute to the beauty of life itself. You will... because you have been blessed.

As you journey through life, I hope you will learn much about your parents and grandparents and ancestors. Your bloodlines flow with honest, creative and enterprising relations. And suitably, this blood will flow through you just as it has passed through your sisters.

Oh, my dear, it is a heartening event when a grandmother can see her grandchildren happy and content. And in this joyous spirit I say welcome, Blessed Emily, welcome to your family.

Love, and thinking of you always,

Curly Grandma

Lady Bugs for Good Luck

> There is nothing like a newborn baby to renew your spirit—and
> to buttress your resolve to make the world a better place.
>
> Virginia Kelley (1923—1994)

One-Year-Old: Picture Book, Picture Book

Many think that toddlers are an unlikely audience for correspondence. Granted, it is one-sided. You will not be getting much in the realm of return letters. But, still, you can send letters to toddlers.

When my grandson, Riley, was around thirteen months old, I wanted to write him letters that he could actually hold in his hand and read. Impossible for sure, but he loved books, and he loved pictures. So, instead of writing him a letter, I wrote him a book (a picture book) a photo album.

I spent a dollar on a little vinyl album booklet that holds around 40 4x6 photos. Riley came to visit me, and I took plenty of pictures. Once the film was developed, I put a photo into a page of the album and put a 4X6 colored sheet of paper in the page facing the photo. On each colored paper, I printed words that I had heard him say that matched the photo. The important element in this "letter book" is the familiar language. I was sure to take a picture of my house, and that was the cover photo. The finished product was 20 photos with 20 matching pages of text.

You can imagine what the photos were just by looking at the corresponding words. Here is a representation of the "letter book."

GO TO GRANDMA'S HOUSE (FRONT COVER)

HI GRANDMA, HI BABA

WHERE'S THE BABY? WHERE'S RILEY?

HI BABY, HI RILEY

SIT IN THE LALA (swing)

WHERE'S THE BALL? WHERE IS IT?

SEE THE BABY'S SHIRT. SEE THE BABY'S PIGGIES (shoes)

TAKE OFF YOUR SHIRT. TAKE OFF YOUR PIGGIES. PLAY IN THE DIRT.

GET A DRINK, BABY

PIGGIES IN THE DIRT. TAKE A BATH

ALL CLEAN

HERE'S A DRINK, BABY

SIT ON THE TRACTOR WITH GRANDMA

RILEY DRIVES THE TRACTOR.   VROOM!   MOVE DIRT!

PUT YOUR HAT ON, BABY

LET'S GO BYE BYE IN BABA'S TRUCK

BEEP BEEP

TAKE YOUR PIGGIES OFF

You can tell that we spent the week playing in the hose and in the dirt, riding the tractor, taking our shoes (piggies) off, and sitting on Grandma's swing (lala).

Riley loved the booklet. He carried it around everywhere he went. When he and Mama went on errands, Angie tucked it into the diaper bag, and Riley would "read" it while he sat in the car seat. The photos were a reminder of his trip. The words were his words. The memory was never lost. And he still has the book and many more like it.

Later, little brother Bryce found the letter books irresistible, and he loved them just as if he were in the photos. This amazing element of letter books was a surprise to all of us. The younger children in the family take on those books and love them just as if they were the child in the photos. We knew Riley would love the books. But we didn't know Bryce would fall in love with them, also. The important thing is that we write to our grandchildren at very early ages because that is when they bond to us.

Another fun feature about this book is that one day, Riley will be able to look back and see how he talked and thought when he was a baby. He will get to enjoy the book from another view.

This is just one idea for writing to toddlers, but with imagination, it could be adapted to almost any subject. Also, with some tweaking, it could be applied to any age. This idea can also be downsized. A single page with a photo taped or glued to it would accomplish the goal of connecting to the grandchild. Or simply scan a photo onto your letter and write personal words beneath the photo. However you produce them, these photo letters are a simple and fun way to stay up front in your very young grandchild's memory.

Somewhere around two or three years old, children become aware that there is something besides pictures on a page. They spend little time looking at anything but those pictures, but they do show a new interest in getting some message out of print. Think about a two-year-old child bringing his favorite book to you to read. He is expecting dialogue (some discourse) to go along with looking at pictures.

Begin writing friendly letters to this child. These are letters that he can hold and look at while Mommy reads to him. He sees the print and the illustrations, and experiences the emotions tied to the print. He is not an independent reader by any means, but he will demand holding the letter, and he will study illustrations.

Keep the letters to only one page and keep the illustrations simple. Any pictures or decorations should match the text or at least be relevant to the child. For example, if the child loves cars, decorate the letter with pictures or stickers of cars. Focus and simplicity are crucial in letters to toddlers. Use short sentences with references to familiar and contemporary events that the child can relate to or remember. A letter containing five to ten very short sentences, with two or three illustrations, is enough for this age.

Decorating the page with stickers is not a good idea unless you include extra stickers. If I had not actually observed my grandson opening a letter, I would never have realized that he tried to remove every sticker to reuse elsewhere. A sticker signals a toddler to stick something somewhere, and the child will find a way to do just that. So, for everyone's sanity, it is a good practice to enclose extra stickers.

The next four letters are for a one-year-old, two two-year-olds and a three-year-old. You can see different approaches to each age.

Maggie is one, and she sees her sisters getting letters frequently, so I cannot leave her out of correspondence. If her sisters get an envelope, she must have an envelope, too! She doesn't know why, but she knows it is good to get a letter. When I write to Maggie, I include only things she knows and remembers about me. She loves my glasses so I draw a picture of my glasses and lightly sketch the rest of my face. She hears her sisters and cousins talk about Curly Grandma's blue house so that is included. Nothing else is needed. No feedback is required. A half sheet of paper is fine for babies, although eventually, toddlers will want the same size letters as their siblings. It doesn't seem like it would make a difference, but they notice these things.

Hello My Magical Maggie,

See Curly Grandma's Glasses?

Curly Grandma Loves You, Maggie.

Mommy will bring you to
Curly Grandma's Blue House.

*Love And thinking
Of you Always.
Curly Grandma*

Olivia is two, and again, her letter is about a meaningful experience, but, her illustrations are much more detailed. The illustrations reflect what was most fun to her when she visited me. All my grandchildren were fascinated with my glasses and Olivia still likes to wear them, so I draw attention to them. Olivia will soon connect me, personally, to my cartoon image.

Livvy, Livvy, Livvy,

I Love You!
I Miss You!

Remember when Brycie gave you a ride in the wagon?

Remember the kitty at Curly Grandma's house?

See my Glasses?

Love And thinking of you Always
Curly Grandma

Letters do not have to be as brief as the above examples. If the child is a good talker he can probably tolerate more information. And he will probably ask questions about the letter's content. If you have a lot of interaction with the child, then you have many shared experiences. You can write about and illustrate each shared experience, no matter how simple. The toddler gets so excited when he sees himself and his experience on paper! Best of all, he can look at the letter over and over. The following letter to two-and-a-half-year-old Riley is an example of writing about a shared experience.

Notice the very large print. Also note that I focus on and illustrate objects that are important to Riley, such as green goggles and the jeep. And, because Riley expects that I bake goodies when he visits, I closed with that topic. (Even today, Riley tells his mother that I am the best cook in the world because I cook only brownies, pancakes, and peanut butter and jelly sandwiches). This bug stationery might have been a good choice for Riley because he was very interested in bugs, as are all two-year-olds, but it is too distracting for this letter. My illustrations were carrying great weight, and so I should have used simple stationery.

Letter to two-and-a-half-year-old Riley:

8-6-04

Hello My Biggie,

Are you my Baby?
Yes you are!

Did you know that
Curly Grandma
and Baba are at
the yellow house?

Today we went swimming with our fins.
We put our goggles on.
We went to the dock where you were fishing
with us.
 Baba and Curly Grandma put our heads in the
water and we looked at the fish in the water.

After that we got in the jeep.
We went for a ride in the jeep.
It is all fixed.
But now Baba has to paint it.

Bye Bye

I have to go bake a cake.
Bye Bye
I love you. I miss you.
See you soon,
Curly Grandma

When three-year-old Emily opens her letter she is convinced she knows exactly what it says. It does not matter that she can't read. She knows the print contains a loving message from her grandma. She holds it, studies it, and "reads" it to Mommy. Eventually, Emily lets Mommy read the real message and the content is discussed. Emily's actions show how fond Emily is of correspondence because she has been receiving letters since birth. It also demonstrates the bonding that can take place between grandchild and grandparent when correspondence begins this early. Notice a question is directed to Emily to employ feedback.

12-04-07

Hello My Blessed Emily,

I Love You.

I Miss You.

I was happy when you came to my house and ate supper with me.

I am glad you liked my Christmas tree.

Will you come to my house again?

Some day we will go to DeFuniak Lake and see all the Christmas lights.

We will see the horse and buggies.

We might even get to see a train!
Bye, bye for now.

Love and thinking of you Always! Curly Grandma

The next letter is correspondence between cousins: Ten-year-old Megan writing to two-and-a-half-year-old Riley. The surprising thing about this letter is that Megan is half a state away from Riley and nearly as far away from Curly Grandma, but from Riley's visits and letters and phone conversations, she knows how much he loves his green goggles. Is it really surprising that Megan uses Curly Grandma's techniques of supporting her letter with illustrations? She illustrates effectively with images that are meaningful to Riley. She also uses the technique of labeling. From reading and enjoying Curly Grandma's letters for many years, Megan knows just how to target her audience.

Ten-year-old Megan writes to two-and-a-half-year-old Riley:

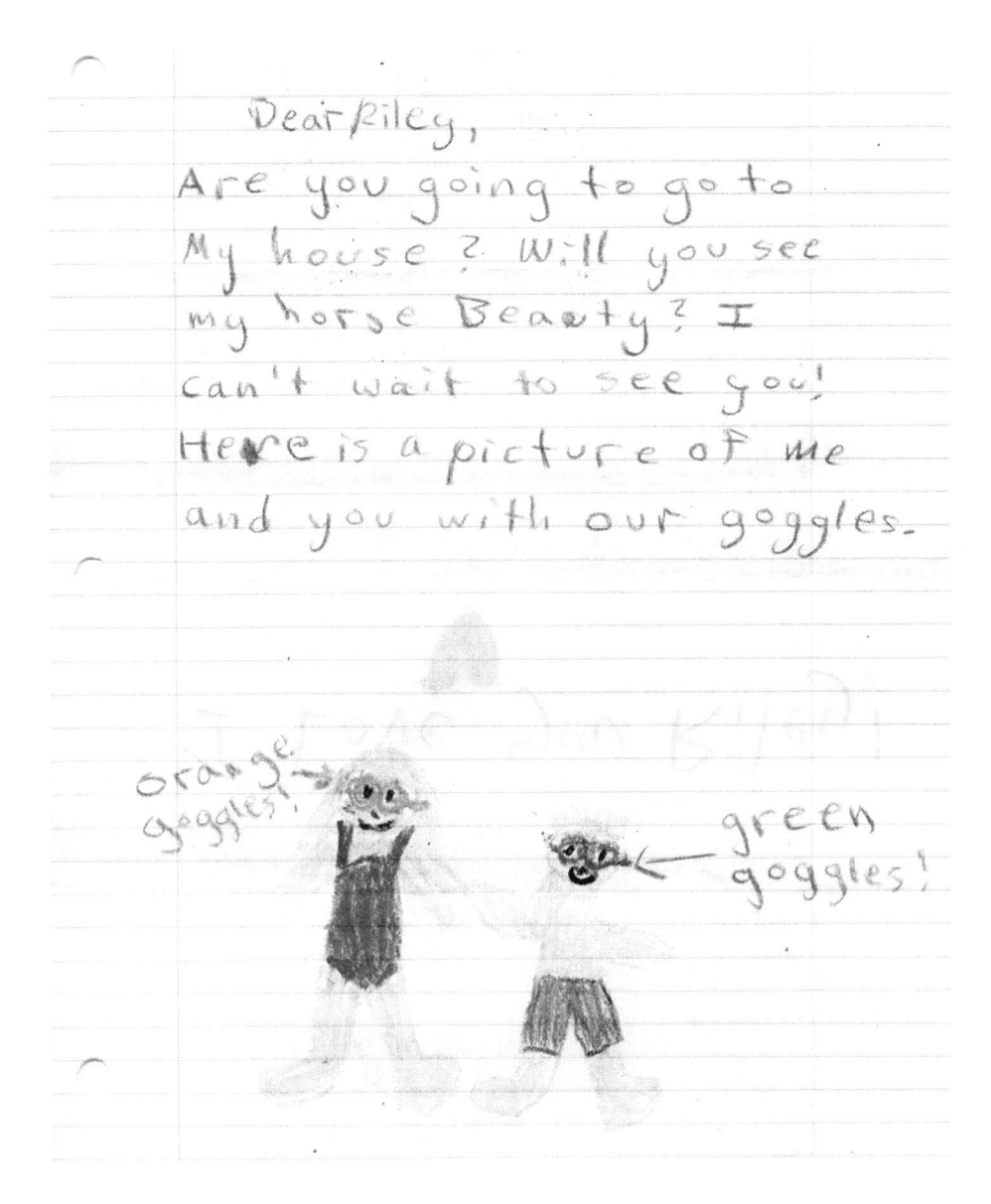

> Dear Riley,
> Are you going to go to my house? Will you see my horse Beauty? I can't wait to see you! Here is a picture of me and you with our goggles.
>
> ← orange goggles!   green goggles! →

Toddlers will not understand autobiographical letters. If the parent is an avid fan of this relationship, you can try writing autobiographical letters because the parent will read and explain. It is the parent who makes an autobiographical letter meaningful to a child who is not an independent reader. However, the primary reason for writing to a toddler is to stay connected. Toddlers have short memories, and we grandparents feel that unless we stay current in their senses in some way, they will forget us. For this reason, you might want to develop a cartoon image of yourself that you draw on all letters and envelopes. You want the child to make a connection to that image as soon as possible. It will become your own logo.

Summary
18 *Months to Three-Years-Old*

- Stick with one page.
- Address the letter with a greeting that you personally use with the child.
- Use language the child hears, not necessarily baby talk, but words that you use in conversation.
- Use very large print, at least 16 or 18 points on a computer.
- Use contemporary content relevant to the child, such as a recently shared event.
- Write only two or three brief paragraphs.
- Write only two or three short sentences in each paragraph.
- Try to include at least one big illustration, preferably two, that match the text, or use simple pictures or stickers.
- Enclose extra stickers for the child to stick.
- Use clean, simple stationery or tape or glue a photo to the page.
- Include a stamped, self-addressed envelope and stationery for a return letter.
- Come up with a cartoon illustration of yourself that you can use as your logo on all correspondence.

A baby is God's opinion that the world should go on.

Carl Sandburg (1878 -1967)

Read Aloud Letters
Transitional Audience
Four To Six Years Old

Four and Five Years Old
Preschool, Kindergarten and 1st Grade

Preschoolers are interested in print and the message that it carries. Some four and five-year-olds are actually reading. They realize that the print is a message that tells the reader what to say. The message stimulates them, and they begin to question the message and carry on a conversation with other readers about the message.

You can write longer letters to preschoolers because you are still writing read-aloud letters. You can combine topics in a letter for this age. Four-and five-year-olds have continuity from one letter to the next. As far as length of a letter, my experience shows one page is great, two can be comfortable, three can test patience, and four may be too much simply because some four and five-year-olds have short attention spans. Length really depends on how Mom and Dad feel about correspondence. If the parent loves this letter stuff, any number of pages will turn out to be perfect. If the parent finds reading the letters a burden, one page is too much. So, get Mom and Dad on board as soon as possible.

Four-and five year-olds are also looking for illustrations to match and enhance the print.

Therefore, illustrations should generally carry out the message in the letter. But, four and five-year-olds understand the difference between illustrations supporting the main message and supplemental images that have been interjected for entertainment, so you can begin to take great liberty with illustrations at this age. You can add stickers, isolated facial expressions, vertical messages, or questions in the margin.

The next letter is to four year old Bryce. Like most four-year-olds, he is learning his alphabet and numbers. Bryce's letter supports the connection between text and images by placing little pictures next to words. He's not able to read this letter by himself when he first receives it. But, after his mother reads it to him, and he goes back to it, he knows what the message says and then he will be able to read it. He will read it the way he remembers it, which is just fine for this age.

In Bryce's letter notice the subtlety of dividing a list in half to reinforce that five plus five is ten, something four-year-olds are learning. Notice the numbers are a different color and in bold for easy recognition. Breaking the list in half is also easier on his eye.

Hello My Brycie,

Did you know I ♥ love you?

Did you know I miss you?

Did you know I hope you come to my blue house again?

Things we will do when you come:

1. Eat ice-cream floats
2. Ride the jeep
3. Read books
4. Play with the train
5. Go to hot chocolate park
6. Eat pancakes with snow
7. Ride bikes
8. Watch cartoons
9. `Play Crackin!`
10. Walk in the woods

So many things to do!
How many things?

Are you playing with your trains?

Come and Visit Me!

Love and Thinking of you Always, Curly Grandma

"Sometimes, it's best to keep things simple."

A good technique in a long read-aloud letter is to address questions to the child. As Mommy reads the letter, the child hears the question and answers Mommy. These questions assure that the child is taking part in the letter even though someone else is reading it.

Another technique is addressing the child by name in the letter. The child's name stimulates interest and acts as a reminder that the letter is not Mommy's letter: It is the child's letter, even though Mommy is reading it. In a read-aloud letter, you can still control the vocabulary.

The following autobiographical letter is a read-aloud letter to Hannah Marie Salzlein, approximately four years old. The bug stationery is a good choice because Hannah spends all her time running around barefoot, keenly scouting for every available insect, amphibian, or small mammal suitable for capture, observation, or domestication. Her mother simply follows a frenzied trail of clothing, shoes, and assorted toys, to find and drag Hannah in for lunch—or for reading Curly Grandma's letter. So, creature stationery fits.

The only reason this letter was four pages was because Hannah's sister was getting a four page letter, and Hannah wanted her letter to be just as "big" as Megan's. I chose this letter to demonstrate how read-aloud letters can be long and still work at this age. Unfortunately, it also demonstrates how Curly Grandma paid no attention to paragraphs and punctuation in read-aloud letters. Had I known I was going to write a book at the time of writing this letter, I would not have made one paragraph two pages long!

Read-aloud letter to four-year-old Hannah:

THE SUMMER BUGS NEVER GO AWAY! THEY BOTHERED ME ON THE WAY HOME FROM SCHOOL AND THEY BOTHER ME NOW!

My Sweetie, My Sweetie,

Thank you for your letter. It was a wonderful letter. It made me feel like I was visiting with you. Now, I don't miss you so much because if I miss you, I just take out your letter and read it over and over again.

My Sweet Hannah, I was very proud of you for saving Domino's life. It's lucky for Domino that you were there to act quickly and get that stick out of his mouth so he wouldn't choke!

My goodness, do you know, Hannah, that your story of Domino reminds me of a time when I was a little girl. I think I shall tell you a story of a time when I saved one of my sisters.

who melted?

Well, long ago when I was about 10 years old, I had to walk home from school. My mother couldn't drive a car to pick up her children from school. Do you know who my mother is? Yes, Grandma Lewis was my mommy when I was a little girl. Well, you know I wasn't the only little girl walking home from school. 4 of my sisters walked home with me. We would be so very hot when we walked home. The sun would shine and, Hannah, I thought I was going to melt into a puddle of syrup!

we didn't have backpacks, we had book bags!

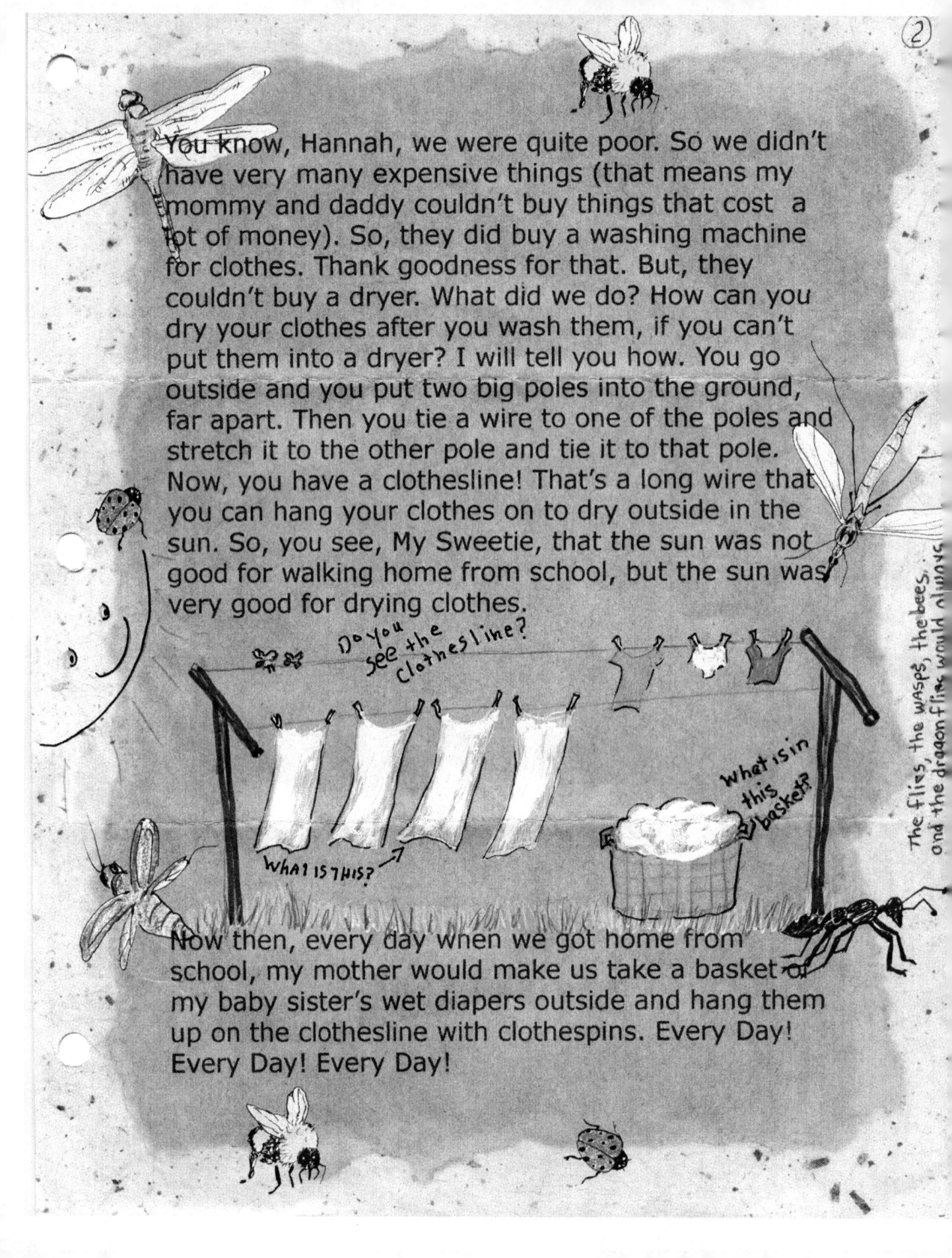

You know, Hannah, we were quite poor. So we didn't have very many expensive things (that means my mommy and daddy couldn't buy things that cost a lot of money). So, they did buy a washing machine for clothes. Thank goodness for that. But, they couldn't buy a dryer. What did we do? How can you dry your clothes after you wash them, if you can't put them into a dryer? I will tell you how. You go outside and you put two big poles into the ground, far apart. Then you tie a wire to one of the poles and stretch it to the other pole and tie it to that pole. Now, you have a clothesline! That's a long wire that you can hang your clothes on to dry outside in the sun. So, you see, My Sweetie, that the sun was not good for walking home from school, but the sun was very good for drying clothes.

Do you see the clothesline?

What is this?

What is in this basket?

The flies, the wasps, the bees, and the dragonflies would always

Now then, every day when we got home from school, my mother would make us take a basket of my baby sister's wet diapers outside and hang them up on the clothesline with clothespins. Every Day! Every Day! Every Day!

Now, here is something else that is different. Today we buy diapers at Walmart or any store. When I was a little girl we had diapers that were like dishtowels. When the baby peed the diaper, we didn't throw it away, we washed it, we hung it on the clothesline to dry, then the baby used it again, and again, and again. We washed those diapers many times. It seemed like we washed them 100,000 times!

HOT SARAH   COLD   HOT ME

It just so happens that on this day my mother gave us some ice cold watermelon to eat first. My sister, Sarah, and I ate watermelon until out tummies were going to pop! Finally, my mother said, "If you don't hang those diapers on the clothesline, you will get a spanking!" You know, Hannah, if we wait too long the rain will come and then the diapers won't dry. So, we ran out to the clothesline, but we were still eating watermelon. We ran to the clothesline with our watermelon. We stopped at the clothesline and Sarah wasn't talking. She was coughing. She was coughing and coughing. She was holding her throat and her face was very red! What was happening to Sarah? Sarah was choking on her watermelon because she ran to the clothesline with a mouth full of watermelon! What could I do? I quickly reached down, way far down into her throat and pulled the watermelon out of her throat. She fell down to the ground, but now she could breathe. I saved her life just like you saved Domino's life.

LUCKY SARAH   LUCKY DOMINO

Isn't that something? Both you and I saved someone's life! You are a smart little girl to think very fast by pulling that stick out of Domino's mouth. I am very proud of you!

I hope you continue being smart and brave forever and ever. I hope you continue helping animals and all people forever and ever. I hope you always try to do nice things forever and ever. Because you are My Sweetie, My Sweetie and You are very special.

I must go now, and put a basket of wet clothes into the dryer. Thank goodness I don't have to take them outside and hang them on a clothesline, because it is already dark outside and there is no sun to dry them!

I love you and I think of you always,

XXXOOO

Curly Grandma

WHY ARE THESE ANIMALS SO HAPPY?

BECAUSE

HANNAH IS SO KIND

Be gentle with the young.

Juvenal Roman poet & satirist (55 AD -127 AD)

Transitional Audience
Five and Six Years Old
End of First Grade

Some children around five years old are beginning to read, and they like the idea of reading independently. They put forth good effort, but tire quickly. Although, they are very limited in their sight vocabulary (words they recognize on sight) and their phonetic skills (sounding out words), they still enjoy trying to read their letters. Letter-writing for this age can be tough but rewarding.

Children in this transitional stage also write wonderful letters with incorrect, but creative spelling that can be decoded. Some professionals call this practice "inventive spelling." An example would be a note that says, "I et rtsv bwlwne." Once decoded, this line reads, "I eat lots of bologna."

This can be a fun age for correspondence because of the puzzling, and even comical letters they write. Consequently, do not underestimate four or five-year-olds as pen pals. Even some very advanced three-year-olds may be capable of this kind of writing. You can expect their letters to be very short, perhaps only one or two sentences accompanied by illustrations. But, their letters truly are a labor of love. However, it would help you if Mom or Dad could send along a decoded version whenever possible.

An example of early childhood writing follows. I think Hannah was at the end of her kindergarten year when she wrote this letter. With it, she enclosed another letter that she wrote a long time ago, when she was little. She recognized her own inventive spelling, and she even seemed aware of the fact that it could not be decoded and therefore, the letter had entertaining value.

Dear curly Grandma this is a pictur of how I rote wen I was Littel. I dont No what most of the things are.

→

FRINDS SCHOOL SCHOOL
NIC
CASE
DISTU
SILEAN
AMI
ANA
ESSa
DiaNa

Five-year-olds are becoming independent readers. This transitional audience is reading part of the letter and having part of the letter read to them.

The next letter to five-and-a-half-year-old Hannah Marie was chosen as an example of targeting the child described above. She is not quite comfortable with reading independently, but she is trying. The real trick here is how I put Hannah at ease. I address some of the letter to her, but I also say, "Maybe Mommy can help you." This lets her know that she is not expected to read her letter on her own, so she is willing to try, but does not feel disappointed if she cannot read independently.

You should notice that in Hannah's letter, I repeat words. This technique is comforting to the new reader and helps to control frustration. It is a strategy that is used in school books for early readers because it employs visual memory. An example of this skill in overkill is in the old primers that read, "Look, Jane. Look. Look at me." It is annoying to adults, but it works for kids. You do not have to go to such extremes in your letters. But, you are looking to aid your grandchild as much as possible, and repetition is an excellent tool for remembering new words.

Another technique applied here is writing only one sentence on each line. The old pre-primers of the Dick and Jane Basils (reading books from the 1950s) also did this. Start a new line for each sentence, no matter how short the sentence is. A struggling reader appreciates this for obvious reasons. Any time you can break things up into smaller pieces, you should.

If possible, keep the sentence shorter than the whole line. If the sentence runs all the way across the paper, the child may have problems getting his eyes back to the left side of the paper and ending up on the correct line. Short sentences may sound choppy to us, but are comfortable to the early reader's eye. They make the print appear clear and the eye doesn't get distracted or lost. This sets up another comfort zone for the child. Also, if Mommy is reading the letter out loud, and the child is following along, he will be able to keep up, easily.

Choice of paper is important for transitional readers. A nice crispy white background helps the reader to stay focused. It is very tempting to use bright or elaborate paper because it is cute or pretty to us, but a busy and bright background could be distracting. Decorative borders are not a problem, but, the print should be on a plain background. It took Curly Grandma a long time (and many letters) to figure out that the simpler the paper, the better off the young reader will be.

At first glance you will notice the glaring problem in the next letter. Paragraphs are too long! There should be only two or three sentences in each paragraph because a beginning reader views a new paragraph as a chance to take a break. There are definitely too few breaks offered in this letter. That second paragraph on the second page is abominable! Too long! And you can see more than one sentence on a line: Not good!

Another problem is that on the third paragraph of the first page, there are too many star stickers running into the print. This causes distraction and confusion. For second graders and older, this would not be an obstacle. But, our beginning readers will certainly feel some stress when confronted with all those stickers so close to the print. The use of stickers on the second page is an improvement.

    Note to the reader: Copyright permission could not be secured for the stickers. I had to remove the star stickers and the smiley stickers and redraw the images.

Letter to five-and-a-half-year-old Hannah:

My Sweetie My Sweetie,

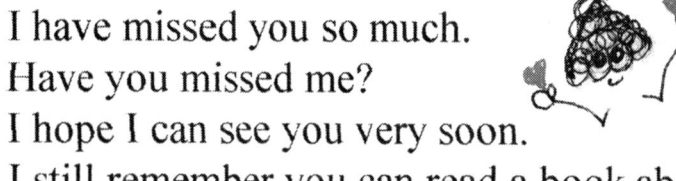

I have missed you so much.
Have you missed me?
I hope I can see you very soon.
I still remember you can read a book about Nala.

Maybe you can read this.
Maybe Mommy can help you read this.

I have been very busy.
I have been helping Aunt Angie with her home.
We have been working very hard.
We made a new floor for her.
We had to glue it.
It is all wood.
We painted her home.
We made a new crib for Baby Bryce.
We did fix a room for Baby Bryce
It was hard.
But, it was fun.

We did a lot of work.
But, we got to play, too.
I got to play with Riley.

Riley is 2.
He is funny.
He can't say Curly Grandma.
He says "Turdy Drama".

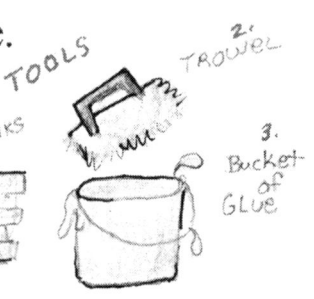

Riley says funny things.
He says, "See what happens" when he falls.
He says, "Let's see" when Mommy tells him, no.
He says, "Now" a lot.
Aunt Angie says, "No Riley, you can't say, now".
But he says "now" anyway.
He says, "I need it, now".
Aunt Angie looks at him and says, "NO!"

Oh well. That's Riley!
Now, Is Hannah happy to go to school?
I hope you are happy.
I think you will be happy at school.
Let Mommy help you read this part.
It is fun to find kids at school to be your friend.
It is fun to find nice kids.
Let Mommy help you to know that not all the kids at school are nice kids. But you can't let them bother you.
You will find the nice kids.
Nice kids will be your friends.
You will have lots of nice kids in your class.
You can be nice to them and
they will be nice to you.
You will help them and
they will help you.
You will have lots of fun.
And you can tell me what you learn.

Well, My Sweetie, I must go now. I love you. I miss you.
I think of you always. Love,   Curly Grandma

Knowing the child personally will help you to style the letter appropriately. Be sure to maintain a good relationship with the parent who can lend a hand in this area. A grandparent who lives far away should take advantage of visits as an opportunity to take out the letters and sit down with the child to reread the letters. The experience will provide great insight in how the child interacts with the letters. It is also a good idea to mail a letter that the child will receive while you are visiting, so you can learn what other kinds of kinks you need to work out.

Let's recap. If you are writing to a child between four and five years old, you are addressing one of two audiences: a child to whom someone reads aloud or the transitional reader who is attempting to read independently.

Read-aloud letters need no specific techniques. Elements such as length, vocabulary, sentence and paragraph structure, and even illustrations are all purely at the writer's discretion. Our guidelines in the box below will apply to the beginning reader.

Summary
Four to Six Years Old
Kindergarten to 1st Grade
Transitional Audience

- Stick with one, possibly two pages, unless the parent will read the letter to the child.
- Choose stationery with a crisp background. Decorative borders are fine.
- Use large print. 14 or 16 points on a computer.
- Double space if the print is smaller.
- Write short paragraphs of two to four sentences.
- Use only one sentence on a line.
- Try not to use the whole line for a sentence.
- Use as many small words as possible, three to five letters, unless the parent will read the letter aloud.
- Repetition of words and phrases works well for this age.
- Content can be contemporary or autobiographical, depending on the actual reader.
- Illustrations should primarily enhance the text.
- Supplemental illustrations or stickers, etc. can be included.
- Questions can be addressed to the child to help focus her while she is reading.
- Include address labels or self-addressed envelopes.

Never have children, only grandchildren.

Gore Vidal (1925—)

US Author and Dramatist

Letter For The Independent Reader

Writing to the independent reader requires some thoughtful preparation and knowledge of the grandchild's skills. As we bond with our grandchild, we will acquire this knowledge, and letter writing will become free and easy. Our best bet in knowing if we are targeting the child's skill level is to ask the parents because they can tell us how easy or how hard it is for the child to read our letter. Parents are a good sounding board and a great resource.

Six Years Old to Eight Years Old
1st Grade - 3rd Grade

A pleasant pastime. *Century Magazine*

Six to eight-year-old children are in first, second, and possibly third grade. They enjoy reading easy material because in school they must read difficult textbooks in their instructional groups, and they are constantly challenged to check out library books in their instructional level. They get few chances to read easy material. A child having difficulty in school will relish a letter he can read with no help. It is like a gift. Children feel good about themselves when they are successful in leisurely activities. Therefore, grandparents should err on the side of simplicity and ease if there is any doubt about the ability of a child in this age group.

Of course you will want to keep the vocabulary simple, but you do not want to sacrifice content and impact. It is just fine to throw in colorful words that require assistance. We do not want to write "down" to a child. We want to balance the message with easy decodable words and the wonderful words that deliver the heart and matter of our letter.

Although there are numerous similarities in a six-year-old and an eight-year-old, there are also many differences. The principal difference is in the time that a six- or eight-year-old can devote to sustained reading. A five- or six-year-old child seems to tire quickly when reading a letter and will often hand it off to Dad to finish if it is more than one page. Unless he is a weak reader, the eight-year-old can sustain long reading periods.

A letter of one or two pages is plenty for a six-year-old. Paragraphs should contain three to four sentences, and the print should be large. However, eight-year-olds are accustomed to as much as six to eight short sentences in a paragraph and they can easily read three or four pages of double spaced, medium to large print.

When it comes to illustrations, the six-year-olds and eight-year-olds have more similarities. The more illustrations, the happier these children seem to be. We do not have to concentrate on large imposing illustrations for this age. Although illustrations should match the general mood or feeling in the letter, this group can easily handle illustrations that deviate from the message. The grandparent can relax and have more fun drawing, placing stickers, or doing any other type of illustrating. Go ahead and get very creative.

The favorite subject for this age group seems to be family. Therefore stories about pets, siblings, cousins, teachers, pastors, and other family topics appeal to them. This is a great time to write lots of autobiographical letters. Of course, media-driven subjects are also interesting to them.

The following autobiographical letter is a good example of how short paragraphs work well for first and second graders. When Hannah received this letter, she read the first two pages by herself, eagerly stumbling through the vocabulary. But on the third page, she was looking for a little help. By the time she got through the first two pages, the long paragraphs on the third page were enough to intimidate her and confuse her. Another problem may have been that she tired after the first two pages.

Letter to seven-year-old Hannah:

My Sweetie, My Sweetie,

10-10-04

It has been a long time since last I saw you.
I do miss you so much.
I think about you and your pets all the time.
I think about your mommy and daddy, too.

Did you notice the letters on this paper?
Did you notice the lower case letter "L" and "I"

They look funny, don't they?
I picked this kind of writing just because it's different.

Well, I hope school is still fun for you. I hope you are still having fun with your friends.

I am so glad all the hurricanes are gone, finally.
That means a lot of the rains have finally stopped.

Here is an old timey song some of us old "cracker" kids used to sing.
By the way, an old Florida redneck is sometimes called a "cracker".

Here is my Florida cracker song. It's a song us kids used to sing when the rainy season is all over.

Oh
It ain't gonna rain no more, no more
It ain't gonna rain no more.

How in the heck
am I gonna wash my neck?

It ain't gonna rain no more!

You see, Hannah, that song implies (makes you think) that Florida cracker kids don't take baths, they just get clean when it rains enough to wet them down.

Sometimes, when I was a kid, I used to *wish* I didn't have to take baths.

We would play outside till dark. We would be so hot and sweaty because we always played chase and hide and seek and jump rope and hop scotch. You know those kinds of games that meant we had to *run* a lot, those were my favorite games.

So, we were very sweaty dirty when we came into the house. That's not too much of a problem for your family.

Don't forget we had only one bathtub for Mom, Dad and eleven kids to share, **not a shower, a TUB.**
How hard is that?
Very hard!

So here is how we did it.
First Dad took a bath, then Mom, then John, then us girls took turns. We didn't have a shower.
So that meant we had to share tub water. And towels!

Here is how we girls would do the baths: I would hurry and take a very quick bath because the water had to be still warm enough for the next girl to get into. I would jump out. Sarah would jump in while I dried off and brushed my teeth. I'm finished, so I go out and Danielle comes in while Sarah is brushing her teeth. Sarah goes out. Now, when Kathy comes in, the water is starting to get a little cold, so she adds some hot water. Now, Danielle goes out and it's time to let half the water out so we can put all four of the babies into the tub and add a little more fresh hot water.

My, My, MY. You have never seen such a bathtub ring in all your life!

But, we all got clean and then we would go out to the living room and watch TV until bedtime.

We would watch <u>The Wonderful World of Disney</u> on Sunday nights.
We would watch <u>The Man From Uncle</u> (a spy movie) on Friday nights.
We would watch <u>The Mitch Miller Sing Along</u> on Saturday nights.
We would watch <u>Bonanza</u> (a cowboy show) on Wednesday nights.
I don't remember too many of the other nights.

My favorite night was Friday. Every Friday night after our baths, Mom would make a big, big pan of homemade fudge. And we would eat the whole pan.(well, not the pan, the fudge).
 I was the happiest kid in the world on Friday nights eating my fudge and watching <u>The Man From Uncle.</u>

Well, I must go now. It is late. I will try to write to you again very soon. I hope you know that I love you and I am thinking of you always.
Love,
XXXOOO

Curly Grandma

One problem for grandparents is if an older sibling is receiving a four-page letter, the younger child also wants a long letter. The easiest solution is to make the print and spacing much larger on the younger child's letter, so they get the same number of sheets.

Following are two letters about the same topic. Each letter targets a different age group: a five and a half-year-old first and then an eight-and-a half-year-old. Notice that there are only five or six sentences on each page of the first letter, but many sentences on the second letter.

Letter to five-and-a-half-year-old Hannah:

Hello to my Sweetie, my Sweetie,
Hello to Hannah!
I love you! I Miss You!

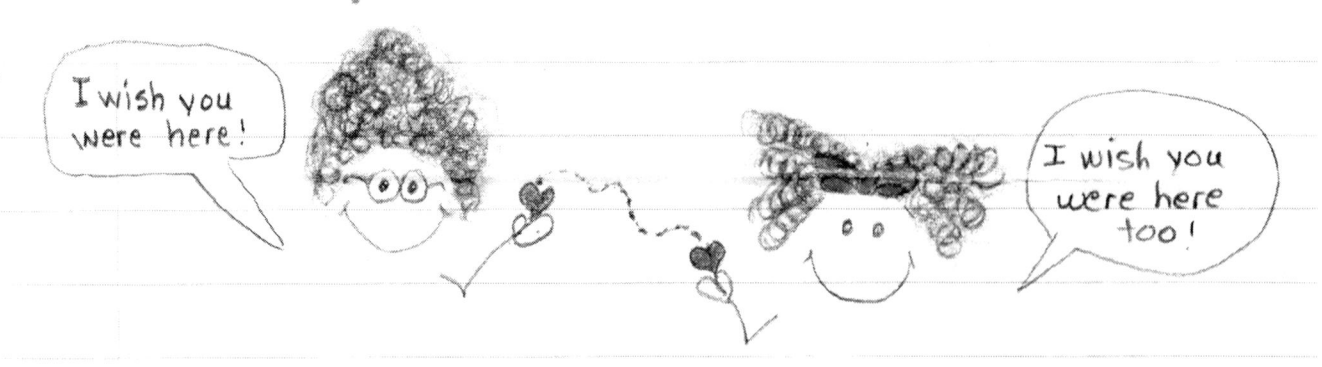

"I wish you were here!"

"I wish you were here too!"

Did you know I moved away from my house?

I live very far away, now.

But I will still come see you!

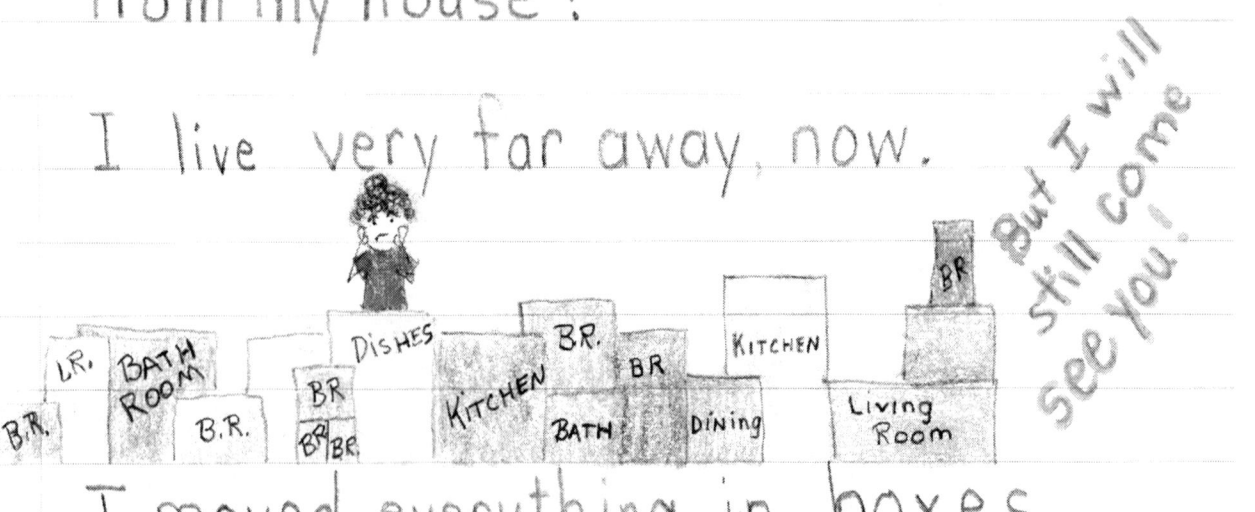

I moved everything in boxes.
Too many boxes!

Here I am in my new home, outside by the lake.

"I'm too old FOR THIS!"

SANTA FE LAKE Mosquitoes (so big!)

SANTA FE LAKE

I have to go now and scratch my mosquito bites!

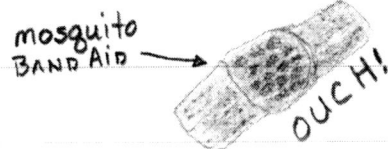

mosquito BAND AID → OUCH!

You be very good, HANNAH! I will think about you all the time!

Who left these footprints on my heart?

Love, xxx ooo

Curly Grandma

Hello to my Dearest Megan,

I have been thinking about you a lot lately. I guess because it was such a long time ago that I saw you last. I have been selling my house and moving. That takes such an enormous amount of time and energy and so I haven't been able to get over to Ft. Meade. Missing you is taking up a lot of my thoughts!!

Poor Curly Grandma!

Lifting! MOVING SHoving! Hoisting! Dragging.

Work! Work! Work!

I'm too old for this!

Moving, as you well know, is a difficult and demanding job. I have carried beds! I have moved couches! I have hauled boxes! I have pushed baskets and pails around and around! I have pulled wagons and hand trucks! I have lifted, lowered, shoved, thrusted, hoisted, and put up, set down, and dragged around more boxes than I ever hope to see again!!!! Can you imagine, Megan? I have 28 years of living boxed up and stashed away in a gigantic storage room. *"Whew"* I am so glad it's over, for now. I will soon have to do it again I'm sure. Because I am only temporarily situated. That means I'm not in my permanent home yet. I'm just renting a house until I find a house to buy. Mommy can explain that a little better for you.

Rent? Mortgage? Buy?

Do you remember when you were moving and Mommy and Daddy looked simply exhausted and drained? Well, that's how I feel. Tired!! But, do you know that I like it? It's fun to work hard towards a goal. It's fun to feel like you're making progress at something you want to accomplish. It's a great feeling to know you're moving along, making adventures, going to new places, seeing new things, meeting new people, and building a new life. But at the same time, it's sad to leave behind your old home, your old neighborhood, your old friends, and to be so far away from the ones you love most.

But I will always be coming back to visit you

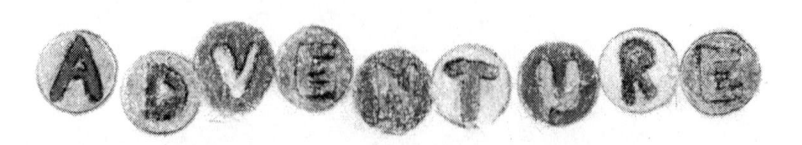

ADVENTURE

I'm sure you felt all of these same feelings when you were moving also. Did you?

1) Megan ...... felt
2) Curly Grandma .. felt

Well I am finally settled into a house on Lake Santa Fe in Gainesville. So, at least I do get to see Aunt Angie, Uncle Mike and Riley a few days a week. My new home is out in the country like yours. And like you, I get to go out and ride a motorcycle (not a 4 wheeler) all around the woods. I ride my bicycle a lot, also. Kayaking and wet-biking are included in some of my activities. I also fish (*not catch, I just can't seem to catch any fish at all*). It seems as though the fish see me and plot together to make sure Curly Grandma doesn't catch a single critter. Not even a tadpole!

shallow CANAL

SANTA FE LAKE
NA NA NA NA NA

She's too old for this!!

Well my Dearest, I must go. I must begin UNPACKING

I miss you! You are in my ♥ always

Love,
Curly Grandma

xxx ooo

The above letter is filled with long sentences and long paragraphs. An eight-year-old who is a good reader can get through this letter just fine. Some of the vocabulary is tough for an eight-year-old who is a weak reader. So, we must know our grandchild. We do not want to frustrate a child with difficult vocabulary in a letter that is supposed to be fun.

Summary
Six Years Old to Eight Years Old
1st Grade - 3rd Grade

Some things to keep in mind while writing to this age group are:

- The child is an independent reader and may want to read letters silently before sharing with the family.
- Length should be one or two pages for six-year-olds.
- Length isn't a problem for the eight-year-old.
- Stick with short paragraphs; three or four sentences for six-year-olds, four to eight sentences for eight-year-olds.
- Use a story in your letter.
- Tell lots of biographical stories.
- Use folk tale or story book language.
- Use simple language, but do not be afraid to use colorful, unusual or "big" words for emphasis. (See *Chapter 4: The 4 Es*)
- Use explanations or clarifications for big or new words.
- Illustrations are a must. They are well loved.
- For six-year-olds, include address labels and stationery.
- For seven-year-olds, include the same, but cut the labels into strips so the child can affix them in the correct order as a learning experience.
- Eight-year-olds enjoy the labels, but they are capable of addressing an envelope.

Eight Years Old to Eleven Years Old
3rd Grade - 6th Grade

Children in this age bracket have varying degrees of reading comprehension. Knowing the child is the only way of targeting their skill level. But all children of this age love long detailed letters (two to six pages) chock full of new words (with some form of explanation). Rich language is a real treat for this age.

This child is discovering how to master writing in school, so they are very observant of our style and content. Folk tale language (explained in the previous chapter) appeals to them. They love the concept of getting a story in a letter, and they want a complementary illustration on each page. A letter about our childhood that employs folk-tale phrases such as "Long, long ago" or "In a time when computers were yet to be discovered" is especially intriguing to them. It also seems that the more brothers and sisters or cousins involved in the story; the better the child likes it. This is an easy age to target, and it is probably the most fun because you can relax while writing to this child.

Summary
Eight-Years-Old To Eleven-Years-Old
3rd Grade - 6th Grade

For this age group we want to consider the following:

- They are broadening their interest outside the home so our topics can vary.
- Letters can be long, up to several pages.
- Paragraphs can be lengthened to several sentences.
- We can write our letter in story form.
- Biographical letters intrigue this age group.
- Language should be rich.
- Use colorful and new vocabulary
- Use many different forms of defining the vocabulary (parenthesis, dashes, repetition, rewording, etc.)
- Children in this age group retain the information in our letters and can recall that information for future letters and discussion.
- These children still enjoy our illustrations and they will begin using detailed illustrations in their return letters.
- Children of this age will pay close attention to our writing style and they begin to copy it.
- Include return stationery and a stamped envelope. Let the child address it for practice, although a kid will love using address labels regardless of age.

Twelve Years and Older
6th Grade, Middle School, and High School

In some ways reaching these children can be our greatest challenge. If our grandchild is difficult or self-conscious, we may want to present letters in a more grown-up manner...but not necessarily.

While teaching eleven to thirteen year old students, I found they loved folk tales, such as Aesop's Fables, just as much as my second graders. At first, the older students tried to be coy and act uninterested. But their interest level and comprehension scores soared with these folk tales even when the reading material was presented on their instructional level. More amazing to me was how they could excel in subjects such as Greek Mythology, which contained difficult vocabulary and high level concepts. The material was complicated, but the language was elegant and the stories were mystical. The students could not get enough, and they would sit and listen to me read these myths aloud to them just as if they were first graders. The language captured them. Therefore, in our letters, we must strive to integrate vocabulary that is elegant, challenging, and stimulating.

One time as I graded reports and returned them to the class, I presented their grades in a sentimental rhyming letter telling them how much I appreciated their hard work. I even put stickers and stamps on them just as I used to do with my first graders. All my students were thrilled with the letter. I saw no scoffing, and several students (girls) told me they would never throw the letter away. Although the boys were not so vocal about their appreciation, I did not see the letters in the trash can, which was common for some students. From this experience, I think you should not underestimate the pleasure a teen will get out of correspondence, no matter what style you use.

Children around this age are going through great changes and yes, some will probably change the manner in which they correspond, but usually it is just the topics that change. The important thing is that you do not get your feelings hurt if you sense aloofness or arrogance, because these children will pull back emotionally if they feel unsure about themselves. What you see as indifference, might really be uncertainty. Maintain a good relationship with the parents, and do not give up on the child. They will usually come around to you again.

These children are a challenge because they are fragile, and their spirit is easily broken. They are sensitive and insensitive. They will surprise you with their wisdom, and they will stupefy you with their senseless and spontaneous foolishness. But, they love correspondence.

Summary
Twelve Years and Older
Sixth Grade, Middle School, And High School

- These children are struggling with peer pressure.
- They still enjoy illustrations, but they also enjoy quips, quotes, riddles, and thought-provoking comments scattered throughout the letter, around the border and in the margin.
- They can enjoy a series of letters without losing the sense of continuity.
- They love humor.
- They are also interested in serious subjects.
- They are immersed in media-driven topics and love sharing information about their favorites.
- They still love a good story.
- Folktale language such as "Long, long ago" is still a great hit with them.
- They may enjoy flirting with poetry or other forms of literature in their letters, so try to be open to experimenting with these genres.
- Because they are exhaustively tested in writing, they observe your writing style and techniques and employ them.
- They will embrace your techniques quickly, and experiment with new techniques: You might feel pressured to be creative.
- They enjoy being outrageously creative.
- Continue to include stamped envelopes for return letters because the child may not be able to secure them.
- Try using emoticons or other computer generated symbols.
- Don't forget that they love correspondence!

Keep in mind, it is not crucial to the success of the letter to implement these techniques, it is just helpful to the child. The real success of the letter lies in the subject content, the feeling projected in the letter, and the anticipation and excitement that is generated from correspondence. Even if you decide not to use any of these suggestions or techniques, pick up the pen, sit at the computer and write. Write lots of letters! You just might get an invitation to join a writer's club.

Harper's, Vol. 48

11-28-04

Dear Curly Grandma,

It's been a long time since I've written. I really miss you. I can't wait 'till you visit again! We can stay up late doing cross word puzzles and telling jokes! Then we'll eat peanut butter bagels for breakfast with hot choclate. I love it when you come over.

The baby's coming soon! I didn't notice how close it was until a few days ago. Mommy went to a doctors appointment Wednesday and the baby already weighs 6 lbs. and 6 oz.! **WOW!** Mommy says she's going to be a big baby!! I can't wait 'till she's born! **YAY!!** ←Me

Christmas is also coming soon. Since it's morning time, mommy says we might go christmas shopping. I hope we do.

I decided to give you a Curly Grandma form to fill out. →

CGC
Curly Grandma Club

If you enter the CGC, you'll recieve jokes, drawings, and more with every letter.

Name **Curly Grandma Bryce**
Address **PO Box**
City **Earleton** State **Florida**
Zip **33333** Phone **555-555 5555**

Please send this form back to the following adress with your next letter.

Mt. Pisgah rd. Fort Meade FL 33333

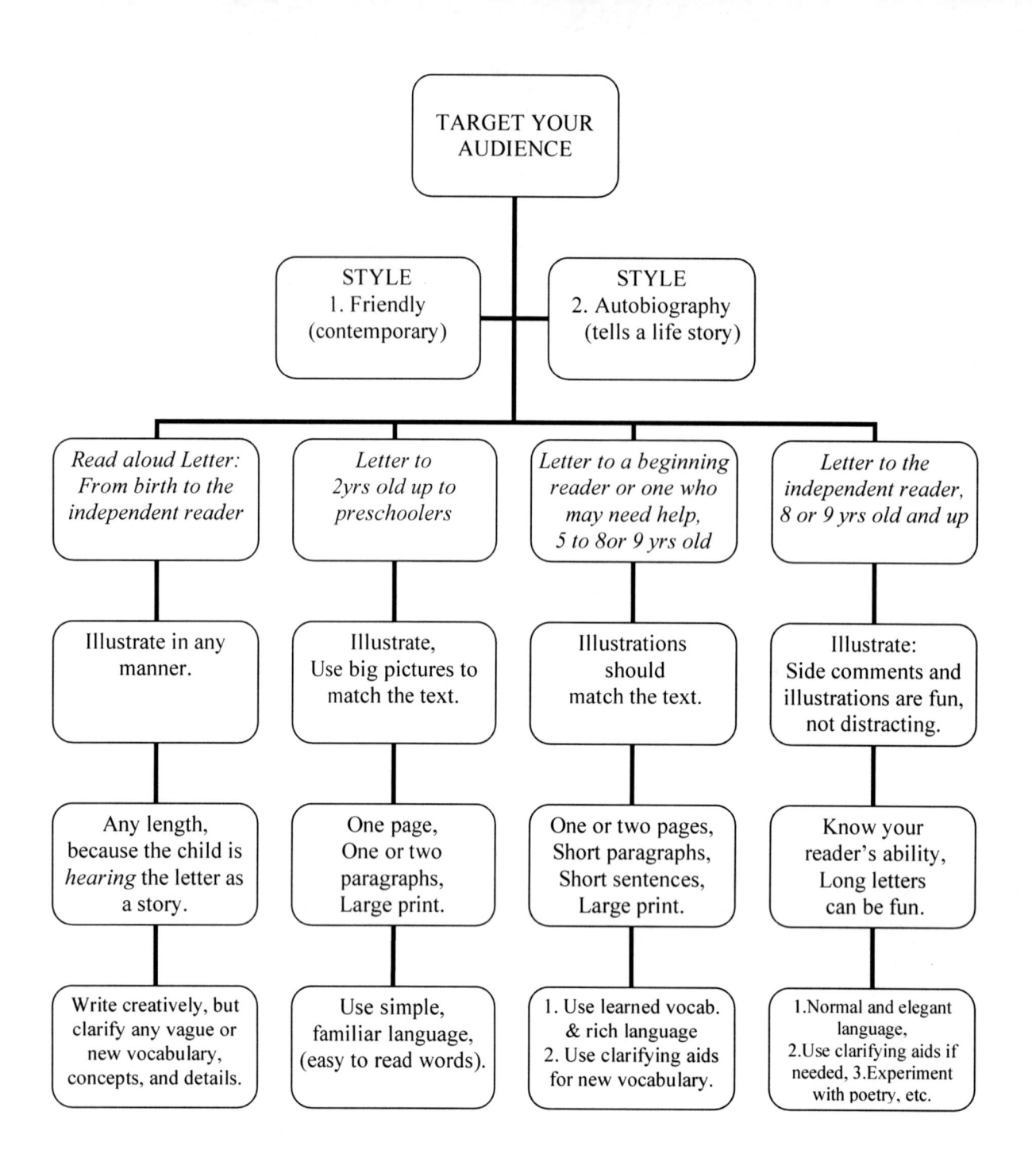

```
                    ┌─────────────────┐
                    │ TARGET YOUR     │
                    │ AUDIENCE        │
                    └────────┬────────┘
              ┌──────────────┴──────────────┐
      ┌───────────────┐              ┌───────────────┐
      │ STYLE         │              │ STYLE         │
      │ 1. Friendly   │              │ 2. Autobiography│
      │ (contemporary)│              │ (tells a life story)│
      └───────────────┘              └───────────────┘
```

Read aloud Letter: From birth to the independent reader	*Letter to 2yrs old up to preschoolers*	*Letter to a beginning reader or one who may need help, 5 to 8or 9 yrs old*	*Letter to the independent reader, 8 or 9 yrs old and up*
Illustrate in any manner.	Illustrate, Use big pictures to match the text.	Illustrations should match the text.	Illustrate: Side comments and illustrations are fun, not distracting.
Any length, because the child is *hearing* the letter as a story.	One page, One or two paragraphs, Large print.	One or two pages, Short paragraphs, Short sentences, Large print.	Know your reader's ability, Long letters can be fun.
Write creatively, but clarify any vague or new vocabulary, concepts, and details.	Use simple, familiar language, (easy to read words).	1. Use learned vocab. & rich language 2. Use clarifying aids for new vocabulary.	1.Normal and elegant language, 2.Use clarifying aids if needed, 3.Experiment with poetry, etc.

Don't use words too big for the subject.
Don't say 'infinitely' when you mean 'very;' otherwise you'll have no
word left when you want to talk about something really infinite.

C.S. Lewis (1898–1963)
English essayist and juvenile novelist

Chapter 7

Protocol to Ponder

Writing letters to our grandchildren necessitates some essential principles. Given that grandparents season with discretion and good judgment, it seems almost needless to include the following information, but human nature requires it. Each of the five principles below will be discussed in this chapter.

MODUS OPERANDI:

1. **Involve the parents.**

2. **Although we are writing to children, expect the parents to read the letters.**

3. **Be Generous in Cheer: Lean in Melancholy.**

4. **Writing to our grandchildren is not a time for "airing out the wash."**

5. **This is snail mail, not e-mail.**

1. *Involve the parents.*

No matter how close we are to our grandchildren, they are not ours. That is why we need the parents' support and encouragement. The parents make or break the relationship because the child is very aware of the parents' attitude at the precise moment of handing the letter to the child. The child can tell if the parent is enthusiastic and pleased for the child, or if the parent is bothered by the whole event. It is also the parents who make sure response letters actually get mailed back to us. Therefore, including the parents is the only avenue for assuring success in our correspondence. How do we get the parents involved? Talk … Talk to them. Come right out and ask them to be involved. A good bet is that it will be a rare parent who will not cooperate or support grandparents writing to a grandchild.

The following letters are an example of how my daughter, Shannan, was actively involved in supporting my correspondence with four-year-old Hannah. When Hannah wanted to send me a letter, Shannan wrote exactly what Hannah said, even writing the mispronunciations—the endearing characteristic of preschloolers. Then, Hannah "wrote" or drew her letter, and Shannan labeled the artwork as Hannah explained it to her. Finally, when Shannan had time, she threw in her own note to say, "Hi." All three pages arrived in one envelope and what a treat it was.

After reading Hannah's letters, imagine how different they would be if Shannan were negative or disinterested in my correspondence with Hannah.

Four-year-old Hannah's "letter" to Curly Grandma:

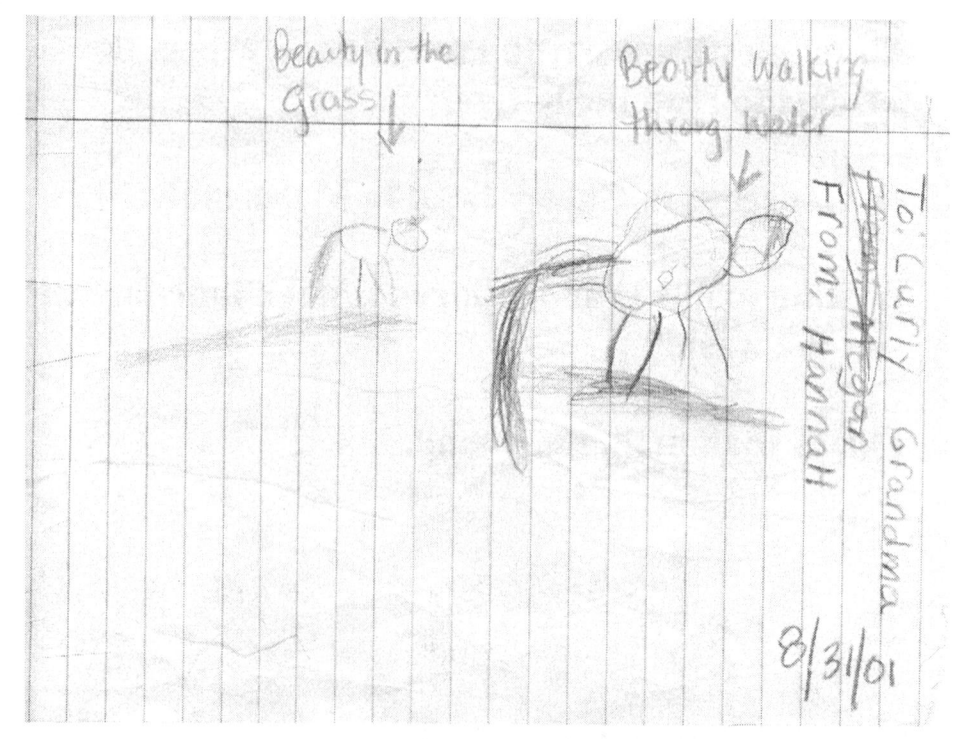

8/29/01

Curly Grandma,

I was tryin' to save Domno's life. BETUZ I didn't want him to choke on this sing.
Domno rides on the yellow 4-wheeler with us alot!
I .. um ...
Curly Grandma, you know how I got the "sing" out? I jus use two sticks to get it out! Then Domno was nice and safe.
Curly Grandma, you know what? We walked Beauty out in the yard and Mommy walked me on the saddle.
Curly Grandma, you know what? I help Mommy clean the bah-room and vaccuum!
Analiese has a kitty named Ki-Ki

I love you sooo much and I miss you.

NOFIN ELSE!

LOVE,
HANNAH

2. *Expect that our letters will be read by the parents.*

Certainly, we should have invited Mom and Dad to be involved in our correspondence. Do not assume that letters pass through the parents' hands unread. The letters may belong to the child personally, but discretion belongs to the parents. Here is how the whole scenario should play out for young children: When the child receives a letter in the mail, the parent gives the unopened letter to the child. The child opens it, examines it, and takes time to get his fill of "It's mine." Then the child asks the parent, "What does it say?" and the parent reads it aloud. As for older children, Mom gives the letter to the child as she sees fit.

> **Note:** Grandparents should never feel uncomfortable with parents reading their letters. Parents always have not only the right, but the responsibility, to stay informed of any relationship the child has with anyone, including grandparents.

Once children reach the age of around eight or nine years old, they begin to view the letters as personal and begin to read them silently, and sometimes do not even share unless prompted by the parents' curiosity.

When I was a child, I could not wait to read my letters to Mom and to my family. As I aged and matured, I did not think anyone was really interested except my mother. I continued to share my letters with her, but did not subject my siblings to the letter's contents unless they demonstrated some interest. Getting letters was a treat, and like goodies, it was better when shared.

3. *Be Generous in Cheer: Lean in Melancholy.*

Of course, we will make our letters positive and cheerful. As for young children, we will not be writing to them about our problems, world peace, war... You get the picture. We want to provide good, interesting, and even fun stuff for them. We want them to look forward to our letters. Letters written in a light-hearted spirit are much more appreciated by a child than the melancholy tone. A child's psyche is fragile and must be protected and nurtured with kindness and resourcefulness.

However, grandparents enjoying a close relationship with older or mature grandchildren can relate sad events cautiously. Understanding the nature of the individual child and his ability to tolerate distressing subjects is extremely important when communicating melancholy issues.

This book is filled with examples of cheerful, happy letters. Therefore, the following letter is an example of a sad subject, and it is written with personal sorrow, but with restrain.

This letter was in response to ten-year-old Megan's interest in the spiritual world. Megan was reading a book about hauntings and spirits, and she had written me a letter about some of her apprehensions, sadness, and fears. She had also talked to me on the phone about the book and her emotions, and so I knew we were on safe ground with this correspondence. I think we can agree it is an honest, but reserved letter.

Letter to ten-year-old Megan:

Feb 26 is a cold and dreary day in Earleton.

Dearest Beloved,   Feb 26, 2004

It was a delightful chat we shared on the telephone the other day. I thoroughly enjoyed the information about your St. Augustine book. The story you told sent shudders up and down my spine, because I too, once experienced a similar haunt. I have often wondered if other people experience haunts and never tell about it or if haunts are just not that much of a regular happening. Nevertheless, I have to share a haunt with you.

As you know, I was a child in a family of 11 children. So all time and attention with Mommy and Daddy had to be shared and that kind of time came in little bites. There wasn't a lot of it available. If something sad or depressing happened to our family, we usually all talked about it together. We would all sit around the table and each of us would chime in our feelings or our questions. Usually, I could be quite greedy about taking up a lot of the talking time. I was teased a lot about talking too much and never shutting my mouth. Now that I am an old lady, I wonder if I was unreasonably greedy and caused my siblings some distress. At any rate there was one incident when I wouldn't talk because I was too, too sad. I was too, too heartbroken.

You see, My Beloved, we had an old white mutt. He was actually a black and white spotted dog sort of resembling a mix of many breeds. We couldn't tell what kind of dog he was. But he was of the noblest and gentlest nature. He was the dearest and most beloved friend a child could have. I am ashamed of how I treated him at times. We kept him tied up out back most of the time and I know I didn't visit him enough. I can't remember how many times we argued about who should take his evening meal out to him. Oh, how I wish I could take an evening meal out to him now. But now is now and then was then and all the wishing in the world won't change things, ever. So, my sweet, sweet Laddy was always there to play with us. He loved to chase us and lay around in the shade on hot days and he loved to play in the hose with us. These were all wonderful things to do with him.

But Laddy could also cause us kids some kind of anguish. You see, like any dog who lives with a big brood of kids, he didn't like it when we left to go to school. He got lonely. So, he would break his rope and follow us to school because we walked to school and he could smell our trail. It was a long way. It must have been about 3 miles. But, he could always find us. We would be in the line going into the classroom and here would come Laddy. He would

I wish I could wish upon a ★

FOOT PRINTS ON MY HEART

Mary had a little lamb
Anita had a little dog 🐕 🐕 🐕

run right up to us and start licking our hands and he would push his nose into our skirts or pants. So there was no question he was ours. We would deny it to the other kids, "NO, I don't know that dog!" But everyone could tell he was OUR dog. Because he loved us so, and he was so happy to see us. Even this situation wasn't too bad, though. The bad thing is that he would sometimes get warts all over his mouth, big ugly warts. Now, if he had those big ugly warts on his mouth and he showed up at school and started licking our hands, all the kids would go, "OOOH, look at that dog!" "YECH!" Now, that was terribly embarrassing. And of course we couldn't deny that he was our dog. All the kids remembered him from the many times before when they had seen him.

Laddy was such a wonderful friend to us kids. When my baby sister, Kathy, would be upset and sit on the back steps crying, Laddy would come over and sit right next to her and cry with her. "OWOOOOO", he would wail and cry like a little wolf in the moonlight. All of us would fall down hysterically laughing and laughing.

Oh, Laddy was such a wonderful dog. And I am sure you know that all wonderful dogs in old stories have to die. And he did. I was devastated. I was so terribly sad and I could find comfort in no one.

As our family was dealing with the grief, I tried to be brave and I tried not to show any tears. But this was impossible. And I remember being embarrassed when my brother looked at my streaking face. So, I slipped into my bedroom and lay down on my bed and cried. I cried and cried and cried. I remember feeling tired from crying and I even remember falling asleep crying and waking up crying. And I could not escape the sadness. My heart felt so much like it really did have a hole in it. I did not want my Laddy to be gone into another place all by himself. My Laddy was looking for us kids, I knew this and I could not find peace because he was missing us. Wherever he was, he was alone. And he needed to find our hand to push his nose into or he needed to have someone to cry with. I had no way of ever being nice to him again. I had no way of helping him ever to come back home. And so my crying could not cease. My mother came in to comfort me, but no, it didn't fill that hole in my heart. I needed to help Laddy and I couldn't. And I cried more and more. As I was laying down with my face in my pillow, I felt my mother come back in and sit down on the bed. I turned to speak to her, but she wasn't there. No one was there except Laddy. Laddy had come back to me. There he was at the bottom of my bed sitting there looking at me with those big brown eyes. So startled was I, that I just sat there looking at him. He stood and then he sat. He started to lick my hand, but he pulled back. We engaged in a very long quiet moment of staring at each other. And then he was gone. But he had come to be my Laddy once more. He came and nobly took with him all my grief and pain. That hole in my heart seemed to fill up and in its place I felt acceptance and relief. Now I could finally quit crying. Laddy had come home. Somehow I knew he was OK.

Oh, My Beloved, I know someone sat on my bed. I felt my bed move when he sat on it. But how? How does a ghost of a dog shake a bed? I will never forget the feeling of the bed move and then seeing no person, only my dog. If I live to be 100 years old, I will always be able to feel Laddy in my heart and on my bed. He was truly a noble friend.

So, My Beloved, when you read me the story about a ghost sitting on the bed, it brought back that old memory of a time when I knew a ghost so well. It brought back a feeling that still brings tears to my eyes. I only hope you have a chance in your lifetime to know a pet as noble and as dear as my Laddy. You too, may one day be telling your grandchildren about a Laddy.

Well, goodbye for now, My Beloved. I hope to be sharing many good St. Augustine stories with you because the Gainesville library has the very same book here. They are going to have it for me in a few days.

Thinking of you always,

Curly Grandma

Curly Grandma

Missing you & wishing you were here

We know that once grandchildren are teenagers, they think they belong in the grownup world and they may begin to change the nature of your correspondence. They become curious about past and present events in the family, and they analyze the future. Thus, the correspondence may demand that grandparents apply some extra caution. If we remember to put the good of the child first, our good judgment will prevail.

4. Writing to your grandchildren is not a time for "airing out the wash."

Grandparents, don't get cheeky. Surely we know that we will never write mean, derogatory, or critical remarks about other family members. Surely we know these letters are not a time for taking sides in the family or bringing up family events that are the proverbial thorn in everybody's side. Surely we know children are to be spared the feuding that comes with familial love. Family is like Vegas—"What happens in Vegas stays in Vegas" and what happens in the family stays in the family. Nobody else needs to know about it and most importantly, the kids don't need to know about it. You do not want to squander a chance to connect with your grandchildren by "airing out the wash" (stirring up family affairs) in your letters. If you have the slightest question about content, do not write it. Indubitably, it does not even need to be mentioned that promiscuous, pernicious, or provocative content and inappropriate language is never acceptable ... for any reason ... ever. Unquestionably, it borders on criminal. Yes, surely we know all of this.

5. This is snail mail, not e-mail.

Oh, the joys of snail mail! It is old-fashioned and in this day of computers (do not say the e-word); it resonates of cobwebs and antiquity. My friends ascertain that snail mail is archaic and possibly verging on primitive. Yes, it is somewhat aggravating when it detours the roundabout passage to ... who knows where? Yes, it certainly can be a bit of an inconvenience, especially when there are two children waiting for letters, and only one shows up in the box. What is a mother to do? It is so ... slooow.

You have to expect problems with mail sooner or later. You have to prepare for differences in mail time. When my family in Lakeland, Florida sends mail to me in Vernon, Florida, it takes at least five to seven days for me to receive it. I am in a very rural area. When I send mail to them, they get it in two or three days. So, plan on these kinds of hurdles when you begin correspondence.

Nevertheless, of all correspondence, snail mail is truly unequaled as tangible proof of one's affections: a triumphant testimonial to fanfare. Yes, snail mail is, above all else, an enduring confirmation of our connections to one another. We letter writers cannot be emphatic enough about the fact that e-mail is not emotional correspondence (although it does have its place in this day and age—think business, think teenagers). But, nothing can replace the excitement that a child experiences when they receive a decorated envelope in the mailbox. Nothing makes them feel more important than seeing their name on that envelope. Nothing can replace this solid, tangible proof that someone loves them and cares enough to send a letter. Yes, snail mail is a joy.

Now, some of my sisters argue my point. In all fairness, they say, e-mail is not only acceptable, but also preferable to many grandparents, especially with older grandchildren. It seems that once a child is a proficient typist, or even a fair one, he seems to get a lot of pleasure out of typing away on a computer and hitting the send button. My sister, Sarah, tells me that while she is working online, she gets many e-notes from her grandchildren. These brief notes do a good job of keeping them connected. But, Sarah agrees with me that e-mails and e-notes don't quite measure up to true correspondence, because they lack the personal intimacy of a letter. E-mail might be okay for note-writing, but snail mail is the only way to go when sending true love or building an autobiography. Something's just not right when a child has to press print to watch a page of your history (or a sentimental letter) spit out of a desk-top vending machine.

Color popping out of the page, opening a decorated envelope and wondering what's inside; even holding a wrinkled, scrunched up letter is not something that can be duplicated in email. Can you send a perfumed letter in email? I think not.

Grandparents, if we incorporate and utilize the above concepts while preparing our correspondence with wisdom and good sense, our legacy will turn out just as we expect; warm, reputable, appropriate, and successful.

> Real integrity is doing the right thing, knowing that nobody's going to know whether you did it or not.
>
> Oprah Winfrey (1954—), in Good Housekeeping

Chapter 8

The Envelope: Or How to Get Along with Your Postmaster

> Neither snow, nor rain, nor heat, nor gloom of night stays these couriers from the swift completion of their appointed rounds.
>
> Herodotus, Inscription, New York City Post Office, adapted from Herodotus Greek historian & traveler (484 BC- 430 BC)

Our postal system works on an automated scanning system. It may be enticing to approach the idea of decorating an envelope like that of icing a cake. However, that approach may cause our postal clerks to look upon us "dedicated epistolary enthusiasts" as less than favorable customers, not to mention the possible delays in delivery it may cause. Even more regrettable is that an unsuitable address or an extravagantly decorated envelope may cause rerouting or worse—a lost letter.

OCR?

Understanding our postal system helps us to address and decorate an envelope without any problems. The automated sorting and reading is done by Optical Character Readers (OCRs). The readers begin at the bottom right hand-corner of the envelope and continue to search in an outward expansion across the envelope, much like a tiny triangle growing bigger and wider.

How the OCRs work:

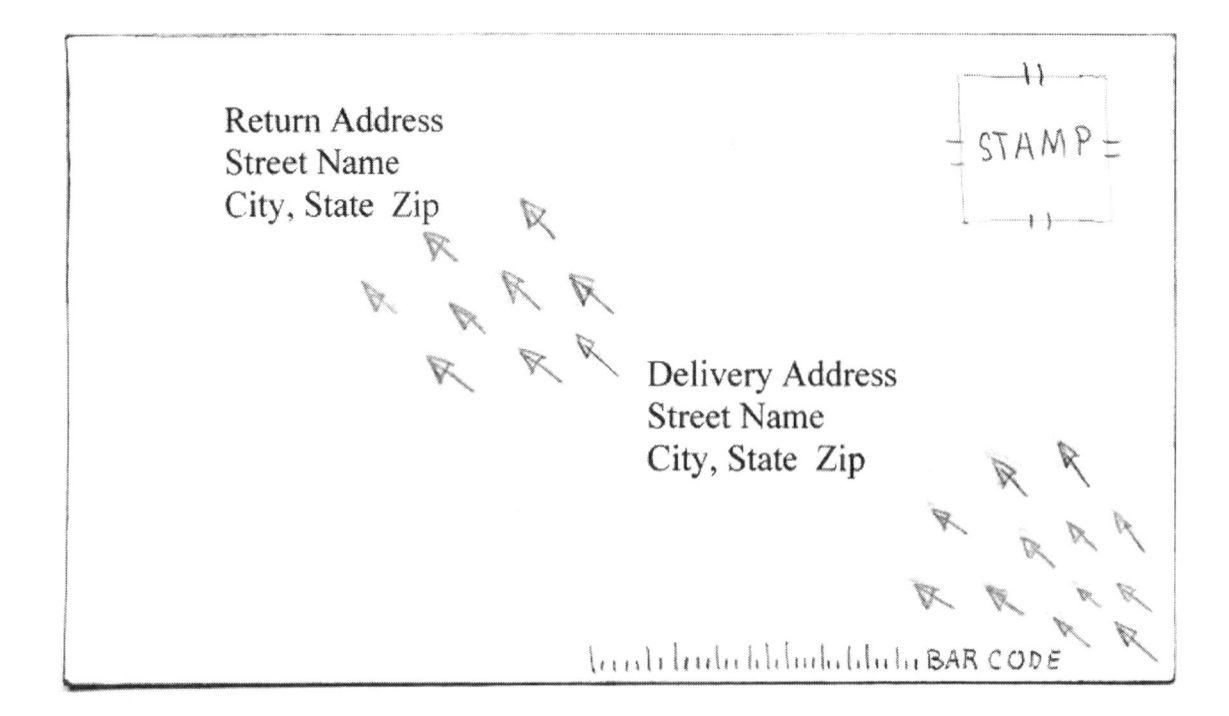

```
┌─────────────────────────────────────────────────┐
│                                        ┌─────┐  │
│   Return Address                       │STAMP│  │
│   Street Name                          └─────┘  │
│   City, State  Zip                              │
│                                                 │
│                                                 │
│                     Delivery Address            │
│                     Street Name                 │
│                     City, State  Zip            │
│                                                 │
│                                                 │
│                          ....||.||.| BAR CODE   │
└─────────────────────────────────────────────────┘
```

The software in the Optical Character Readers is set up to read a full address. It then cross-checks the address against the zip code in the database to determine that it is correct; therefore, a full address is required. A zip code by itself is not sufficient, just as an address without a zip is also inadequate. Illegible addresses cannot be deciphered by the OCRs and will result in delays because the envelope will then have to be removed from the automated system and manually read by a person.

Delivery Address

Begin the delivery address just a little below and to the right of the center. This is the prime spot for the OCRs to read. At one time, it was popular to put the delivery address all the way to the left, but that style is not compatible with the automated system.

Placing stickers above this address is fine, as long as it is not so high that it interferes with the stamp; keep them toward the center. But never place decorations beneath the destination address because that space is used for a barcode.

Return Address

The return address should be in the top left-hand corner. It is fine to drop it down a bit to leave some space above this address for stickers, but we should avoid placing decorations below the return address because of the OCRS.

⬅ Room for stickers

Return Address
Street Name
City, State Zip

Delivery Address
Street Name
City, State Zip

- Try to envision three off-limit spaces for stickers and drawings because:
    1. The area *below the delivery address* will be bar coded.
    2. The area *below the return address* will be read by OCR.
    3. The *upper right corner* is for the stamp.

[Envelope diagram with handwritten annotations:]

Return Address
Street Name
City, State Zip

Delivery Address
Street Name
City, State Zip

3. No Stickers!
STAMP

2. No Stickers!
OCRs travel below the Return Address

1. No Stickers!
Bar Code

The easiest way to keep the Post Office happy is to exercise the idea that we will not put anything below the two addresses. For decorating, we will use only the area above and between the addresses.

Another space that can be utilized with no ill consequence is the back of the envelope. If we enjoy writing little notes or surprise comments on the envelope, this is the safest place. Many times the back of my envelope has been just the right spot for a tongue twister or a brainteaser. The following envelope was just right for three-year-old Bryce who loves trains. For a three-year-old, get big and make the back—the front!

The back of my envelope:

[Envelope with drawing of a train, captioned:]

Hello My Brycie!

Woo Woo Wooooooooo Toot Toot Toot

After many letters, I finally came upon a pattern of decorating that I was comfortable with and one that my post office amicably accepts. The illustration below may give you an idea for a pattern that you can use. The envelope in the illustration is delivering tiny hearts to Maggie and Olivia. However, my images change with each grandchild. Sometimes, my envelope delivers tiny baseballs, horseshoes, stars, pirate flags, or paw prints. This is the fun of personally decorating an envelope—it can be changed according to each grandchild's interest.

My decorated envelope:

P.S.

Why do stickers delight children? I do not know, but children will have stickers flying about and covering every inch of available stationery. It seems that a young child with a package of "something that will stick to something else" can easily be overtaken by some transcendental power. As well as stickers, it appears that tape, labels, and glue also fall into this spellbinding category. Keep in mind your grandchild may require a little help, and possibly some tutoring, before he is safely left alone with an envelope and stickers.

Curly Grandma can attest to this problem first hand as my granddaughter, Megan, once mailed me an envelope with a balloon attached to the back. What surprised me most was the fact that the one stamp was enough to pay for the many pieces of tape she used to ensure that the balloon made the trip. And so it is that I am sheepishly reminded of what a good deal our stamp is.

Nevertheless, I still wonder what kind of language the postal clerk was using when Megan's elaborately decorated letter and its affixed companion was flung from the automated OCRs.

Chapter 9

An Inkslinger's Cupboard

One only needs two tools in life:
WD-40 to make things go
and duct tape to make them stop.

G. Weilacher

Relative to the above quote, the only tools really necessary for correspondence are pen, paper, and stamped envelopes. However, stocking up on some of the following supplies will make letter-writing more fun and convenient. As you read, jot down your own ideas to personalize your cupboard and stay well-organized.

1. Three Spiral Notebooks (Three Rings)
   - Two notebooks for the grandparent: one for saving your grandchild's letters and one for a copy of your letters before you mail them.
     - However, some grandparents prefer all letters in one notebook, filed by date. They like seeing their letter (to the grandchild) saved next to the response (from the grandchild). This method visually maintains the sequence of correspondence.
   - One notebook to give (or mail) to your grandchild so he can use it to save and organize your letters. The handiest is a one-inch vinyl notebook with the pockets on the inside of the front and back cover.
   - Some kind of box or container if you decide to forgo the notebooks.

2. Hole Punch
   - A three-hole-punch is much more convenient than a single hole punch.
     - The child does not need a puncher because you will always punch your letters before you mail them.

- You can punch the child's return letters when you receive them.

3. Reinforcements
    - As soon as you punch your letters, reinforce the holes with sticky circles to prevent them from tearing out of the notebook.

4. Pens, Pencils, Crayons, and Markers
    - Every color and every kind.
    - Gels and metallics and anything else colorful and even unusual.
    - Mechanical crayons work well for coloring small illustrations.
    - White-out or some kind of liquid paper for coloring white things on white paper.
    - Some kind of container to corral coloring tools; a tackle box or small tool box works well.

5. Paper
    - All kinds of stationary: buy the smallest packages because you want a variety of styles, not too bright and with narrow borders because borders can be distracting.
    - Different colors of stationary.
    - Decorate your own paper to make unique stationery.
    - Note cards and envelopes.
    - Postcards.
    - Colored paper (for your own creative ideas and photo letters to toddlers, such as the one in chapter 6).

6. Envelopes
    - Stick with the long legal size: the short ones are inconvenient.
    - Different colors of envelopes.

7. Stamps
    - The post office usually sells a style of stamp that avows, "I love you." Retain regular stamps for regular mail, but use love stamps for your grandchildren.
    - Post card stamps.
    - You can now order stamps with your picture, or the child's picture, or even better, a picture of both of you.

8. Stickers
    - Every kind of sticker you can think of, especially the smaller ones; they fit better.
    - Alphabet stickers for side messages in the margin.
    - Number stickers to include in side messages.
    - Smiley stickers.
    - Tiny foil stickers (hearts, stars, bugs, etc).
    - Small teacher stickers such as *good job*, *wow*, and *fantastic*.
    - Stickers which are particular to your grandchild's interest such as cars, bugs, cartoon characters, etc.
    - Stickers which are particular to you and your interests.

9. Stamp Pads and Stamps
    - Every kind; try to find stamps that parallel your interests or the interests of your grandchild. Holiday stamps are handy.

10. Labels
    - For children who are younger than six, include address labels. The child cannot write addresses on an envelope, but he will love sticking the labels on the envelope. For older children (seven or eight) write the addresses on the label, then cut the label into three different lines so they can piece the address together as a learning process.
    - Even teens enjoy writing the address on a label and decorating it.

11. Models to Aid Us in Illustrating
    - A movable wooden body to model motion and movement
        - See the section Illustrate in Chapter 3: The Heart of Correspondence for sample figures in lieu of a wooden model
    - Facial expressions chart
        - Also in the same section and same chapter is a chart of expressions.

12. Computer? Typewriter? Feather Pen?
    - A computer is the best way to write letters because each letter can be composed, edited, saved, printed, and filed for future reference. Even a computer that is ten-years-old and has basic word-processing and a simple printer will work. Of

course a scanner is always nice to save the letter once it has been illustrated. But, sometimes handwriting a letter is best of all, especially with an antique fountain pen, or if we are real lucky—a feather pen.

- A scanner is also a good tool if you are making your own stationery. With one of these, any drawing or flower can magically appear on your paper.
- An old electric typewriter is pretty handy for typing labels, postcards, and other small stationery if a computer is not possible.

13. Dictionary and Thesaurus
- No matter how good we are at writing, we will need these books; they can solve our word quandaries, and twenty-year-old dictionaries work just as well as new ones.

14. A Copy of All of Your Letters
- Before you mail your letters, copy it for your notebook.

Fifteen cents of every twenty-cent stamp goes to storage.

Louis Rukeyser

We letter-writers tend to have a lot of tools, and we love our tools! Most of all, we love our computers. And, no matter how many times they crash, we continue loving our computers. Even when my attentive little XP-Paper-Clip-Office-Helper rudely falls asleep in boredom or knocks on my screen with "Hey, Dummy! See what you just did?" I still love my computer. With this in mind, I can't help but include the following quote.

If the automobile had followed the same development cycle as the computer, a Rolls-Royce would today cost $100, get a million miles per gallon, and explode once a year, killing everyone inside.

Robert X. Cringely, Info World magazine

Chapter 10
The Benefits of Correspondence

We grandparents reap many benefits from corresponding with grandchildren. It seems that letter-writing promotes good emotional and mental health in seniors. Studies have shown healthy results occur—such as avoiding depression, gaining feelings of self-worth, and possibly even averting dementia—just from writing to our offspring. Many resources support the benefits of writing, and a few examples are offered here.

One of the primary benefits of corresponding is when we write about our everyday activities we are sharing our inner thoughts and feelings, which enhances emotional well being. It has been reported that correspondence is unique because it is meant specifically for the participants, especially the receiver. It is personal and it is proof of affection. Lawrence Martin, in one of his Vibrant Life articles says correspondence provides better health physically, mentally, socially, and even spiritually because it offers us a better outlook on life.

In 1994, Leslie O'Flahaven wrote a warmhearted article "So Much To Say" in EnRoute, the newsletter for the National Postal Museum members. O'Flahaven presented a letter writing program organized by the museum called Across Town Pen Friends. In this program, senior citizens were paired with middle school pen pals for four months. They would meet at the museum, see films, and tour the gallery. Then they would write letters to each other about what they had observed and how they were affected by the visits. A few of the benefits listed for all the participants were a feeling of genuine connection through open communication, feelings of self-worth, a chance to model good letter writing skills and a chance to learn these skills.

A feeling of connection, feeling that you have done something good, and getting a chance to show a youngster how to write good letters—if these benefits result from strangers connecting through correspondence, how can grandparents and grandchildren not enjoy the same benefits?

This postal program continues today and a free curriculum guide is available on their website listed in the references at the end of the book.

Valerie Borey wrote an article in Suite 101 for grandparents. She explains how Norwegian grandparents can use correspondence as a tool to teach grandchildren their native language.

She gives tips and ideas on how to teach their language through fun and challenging activities. This is a good example of how immigrant grandparents in our country use correspondence to share their culture and their heritage. Sharing our history is a good way to enhance our emotional wellbeing, and that is what we do in our autobiographical letters.

A second concept that seems to be echoed in scores of research is that writing about the good ol'times is almost like therapy because reminiscing (recalling the past) acts as an antidepressant. When we write about our past, we not only get to lollygag in old times, but we also record meaningful events in our life. And, when we write about our life, we are validating to ourselves that we have indeed been living well and have a life to share.

The American Geriatrics Society, www.americangeriatrics.org, is devoted solely to enhancing the health of senior citizens. AGS posts many articles on the Web, in magazines, and in newspapers. In an online article, "In Eldercare At Home: Ch 19 Depression," reminiscing is highly recommended as a means to help offset sadness and negative thoughts. It says that telling stories about our childhood and even researching family history could help to stop the negative thoughts that begin the downward spiral into depression.

In the Journal of Clinical Nursing, Cynthia Stinson and Edythe Kirk wrote about a study on the subject of reminiscence. The goal was to find a way to manage depression without using drugs. The study was done in an assisted living facility in Texas, and the conclusion was that indeed, reminiscence could be a possible intervention. I have personally experienced this effect. When I reminisce, a sense of well-being overtakes me and fills me with mild euphoria. Writing letters about the fun I had as a child lifts my spirits, and that feeling can last for several hours, sometimes ... days.

Help Guide: Mental Health Issues posted an article that described the signs, symptoms, and causes of depression in seniors. The article focused on seniors benefiting from self-help activities. It explained how seniors could offset depression by elevating their mood. As expected, the usual walking, music, and pets were prescribed. But, other not so common suggestions were listed. Visiting with family and friends and reminiscing with either young people or other seniors was recommended. Another suggestion was to engage in humor, such as telling or emailing jokes and funny stories. Reminiscing and telling humorous life stories is exactly what we do when we write our autobiographical letters; consequently I think we will be reaping the same kind of benefits.

One more thought is that writing letters also gives us purpose and motivation for exercising our brain. Mental exercise is a challenge that we can meet in a fun and pleasurable manner, and it could help to fend off the mental deterioration that comes with old age according to some studies. In a study that Laura Beil wrote about in The Dallas Morning News, Dr. David Bennett of the Rush Alzheimer's Disease Center in Chicago said that mentally challenging activities could possibly reduce the risk of Alzheimer's.

Letter writing on a regular basis enhances planning strategies and organizational skills. It forces us to think and communicate on different levels, using different vocabulary, and even different literary forms. It also allows our brain to try new things by experimenting with written emotions, ideas, and attitudes. All of this is good mental exercise. Therefore, I think every time we have to stop and search for the right words to write, or when we are forced to use our dictionary and thesaurus, and even when we rewrite, edit, or "cut and paste," we are in fact helping to fight off Alzheimer's. I think this letter writing business is very good for us.

If you have a parent or grandparent who is not capable of writing their own letters because of physical health problems, but you would like to preserve their past, try getting them to dictate their stories to you. Record their stories on tape, and then when you have time at home, write it. This same concept is carried out at Louisiana State University in a program called "Life Lessons: Memoir Writing with Senior Citizens." Psychology students earn credit in a class that puts them in a real-world setting. They interview a senior citizen several times, tape their life stories, add past and present photos, include a biographical sketch, and put together a wonderful memoir for them. The seniors view this as a great treasure, something they always wanted to do for their offspring, but never could get around to doing.

If you decide to pursue the memories of your parent or grandparent, you will be surprised at how much information you do not know, or misunderstand, or have incorrectly documented. This project involves a lot of writing, a lot of time, and a lot of dedication, but it will be worth it.

An online visit to The Legacy Project at www.legacyproject.org can offer grandparents a pleasant retreat. It is a family website that features some very worthwhile books and presents their Across Generations program through free kits and activities.

Here are a dozen reasons for corresponding with your grandchildren:

1. It is just plain fun.
2. It can fill a void when we feel distant or alone. It makes us feel important and loved.
3. We learn and enjoy the value of patience and anticipation.
4. We experience the tangible result of diligence.
5. We experience the give and take in a relationship, and the reciprocating value of looking out for each other while engendering a new kind of emotional connection.
6. We find an avenue for emotional exchange while encouraging and welcoming personal and creative expression.
7. We are challenged to write in new genres and expand our communication skills.
8. We engage in mental exercise and improve our concentration.
9. It motivates us to document our history.
10. It lets us reflect on our past in a positive way.
11. We engage in humor.
12. Most importantly, it connects us with our grandchildren.

So, why is correspondence good for us? Very simply, we are enhancing good health (physically, mentally, and emotionally) by staying connected to family, by actively preserving our past for future generations, and by sharing enjoyable experiences with our grandchildren. But, the real rewards are treasures that cannot be described in words.

In the first month of fourth grade, my granddaughter, Megan, had to write an essay about someone she admired. She wrote about her Curly Grandma. It is both touching and humbling that correspondence with an old lady could have been meaningful to a child. Megan's mother, Shannan, saved the essay suspecting that it might make my day.

> Megan Salglein
> Sept. 15, 2004
>
> The person I admire is my grandma. I call her Curly Grandma because she has really curly hair. My grandma does fun stuff with me and my sister. When I was little, we used to go to Seaworld alot.
>
> Seaworld was really fun. I like to watch Shamu, the Killer Whale. He does good tricks. He can slap his tale on the water and soak half of the audience. There is also a stingray pool. You can touch the stingrays that are swimming around.
>
> My grandma does alot of other cool things. She likes to play with me and my sister. Unlike other grandmas my grandma writes letters to me and my sister atleast twice a month. She decorates these letters with stickers. My grandma is really great.
>
> Grandma You are a special gift. Cherish her always

Ten-year-old Megan was pretty good at writing thank you cards, too. This card is not the usual thank you card. While thanking me for birthday presents, she experiments with writing style and projects her inner self (her voice). She enjoys using language that creates an exotic, Shakespearean or even fairytale ambience. I wonder? Where did she get such pretentious flamboyance?

The envelope:

A card for Madame Bryce From the Salzlein Residents

↑ Official Salzleins' Stamp.

Curly Grandma's Letters · 163

Dearest Grandmother,   5-10-04

I'm very fond of your gifts. I've watched Brother Bear and it's quite a beloved tale. I haven't yet seen Misty, though I'm sure it will be just as good. I've also been using my crayons quite often. I already have my horse plaque and picture frame up I just need a picture to be the center of the lovely frame. Remember, I'm always thinking of you!

Love,
Megan
xxxxxxxxxx
oooooooooo

P.S. How'd you like my new voice?!
:) I love you

Call it a clan, call it a network, call it a tribe, call it a family.
Whatever you call it, whoever you are, you need one.

Jane Howard, (1935–1996) *Families*

Addendum

I love being a writer. What I can't stand is the paperwork.

Peter De Vries

Well, there you have it. Some ideas, techniques, strategies, and one person's opinions. I hope you have been inspired. I hope you agree that brief, fleeting moments of writing or even frivolous pages of correspondence with your grandchild could never be considered pointless. I hope you have found an affectionate, new avenue for offering head and heart to your grandchild.

If you have read this book, and you feel overwhelmed, forget the book. Just write a letter. So much of this information is now embedded in your mind, that you will automatically implement many of the techniques and strategies with very little effort. You do not need this book to tell you how to write from your heart. You love your grandchildren, so write to them. But then, someday, you might think, "My last letter was boring. I need to jazz it up a bit." That is when you grab this book. Sift through a few pages, and you will find your letters energized. Some little technique in the book will trigger a new flair in your letters or maybe solve a little problem. With this book, you will just get better and better; you will be more entertaining, more engaging and more comfortable with correspondence.

What this book does for you is launch a new method of unique communication for you and your grandchildren. It helps you stay connected to them, and it helps you pass on your life history in a fun and creative way. That's all. The real jewel here is that you want to do it. So, you can't go wrong. Therefore…write!

History will be kind to me for I intend to write it.

Sir Winston Churchill (1874–1965)

Resources

Beil, Laura
    "Stretching your brain: Mental activity may help fend off
    Alzheimer's" Improving Everyday Memory in At-Risk Elderly
    Date: 3–25–2002 Publication: The Dallas Morning News
    Page: 1C, 2C (10 September 2006).
    http://www.nur.utexas.edu/fachome/gmcdougall/Documents/DallasMorningNews

Borey, Valerie
    "Grandparents as Tools for Language Learning" Suite 101: Enter Curious
    Published on: May 3, 2002 www.suite101.com (4 November 2006).

Hutman, Sheila, Jaelline Jaffe, Ph.D., and Jeanne Segal, Ph.D., contributed
    to this article. Last modified on 2/20/05.
    "Depression in Older Adults and the Elderly: Signs, Symptoms, Causes and Treatments"
    Help Guide: Mental Health Issues
    Expert Non-Commercial Information on Mental Health and Lifelong
    Wellness (8 December 2006).
    www.helpguide.org/mental/depression_elderly
    © 1996–2006 Helpguide.org. All rights reserved.
    Can also be viewed at:
    www.stanford.edu/group/usvh/stanford/misc/depression
    as USVH Disease of the week #2: Depression in Older Adults

Kemp, Gina M.A., and Cara Rosellini contributed to this article.
    Last modified on 12/27/04 "Humor and Laughter: Health Benefits and Online
    Sources" Helpguide: Active Healthy Lifestyles
    Expert, Non-Commercial Information on Mental Health & Lifelong
    Wellness http://www.helpguide.org/life/humor_laughter_health
    © 1996–2006 Helpguide.org. All rights reserved (8 December 2006).

Martin, Lawrence M.
    "Healthy Words-Letter Writing as Therapy" Vibrant Life; Sept-Oct 1995
    ©Copyright 1995 Review and Herald Publishing Association
    ©Copyright 2004 Gale Group http://findarticles.com (21 November 2006).

O'Flahaven, Leslie
>"So Much to Say" [National Postal Museum Promotes Cross-Generational Exchange];
>Article from EnRoute: volume 3, Issue 4 Oct-Dec 1994
>Across Town Pen Friends, a pilot letter writing program organized by the National Postal Museum http://www.postalmuseum (10 October 2006).

Stinson, Cynthia Kellam & Kirk, Edythe (2006)
>"Structured reminiscence: an intervention to decrease depression and increase self-transcendence in older women." JCN Journal of Clinical Nursing
>15 (2), 208–218 doi: 10.1111/ j.1365–2702.2006.01292.x
>Can be viewed at http://www.blackwell-synergy.com (4 November 2006).

Louisiana State University, Baton Rouge, LA 70803
>"Life Lessons: Memoir Writing with Senior Citizens" LSU Highlights, Spring 2005, Community Partnerships, Contact Rebecca Acosta/LSU University Relations Highlights Team www.lsu.edu/highlights/05 (21 November 2006, 5 August 2007).

The AGS Foundation for Health in Aging
>Eldercare at Home: Chapter 19 Depression
>©1999–2002 The AGS Foundation for Health in Aging. All Rights Reserved http://www.healthinaging.org/public_education/eldercare/
>the American Geriatrics Society www.americangeriatrics.org reached beyond its traditional role as a professional clinical society to launch in 1999 the first national public organization devoted solely to the special health care needs of older adults - The AGS Foundation for Health in Aging. (8 September 2006).

Hart, Harold H., Compendium of Illustrations in the Public Domain, Hart Pub. Co., NYC
>© 1983, compiled by Harold H. Hart

SEARS®, Sears Holdings and Corporate Communications, Historical Archives, 3333 Beverly Road CC-745, Hoffman Estates, IL 60179; Some pictures, illustrations and all catalog items (pens and writing tools) are from the 1987 and 1927 catalogs titled: *SEARS ROEBUCK & CO.*, (Incorporated). *Cheapest Supply House on Earth, Chicago 1987, 1927.*

Quotations

The letters of a person... form the only full and genuine journal of his life.
Thomas Jefferson (1743—1826) US diplomat, politician, and scholar; wrote Declaration of Independence 1776; 1st Secretary of State 1789–1793; vice-president of US 1797–1801; 3rd president of US 1801 -1809

The above quote is from "Thomas Jefferson at Monticello" exhibition, Monticello Visitors Center, Thomas Jefferson Foundation, Charlottesville, Virginia. Printed with permission.

All other quotations are from The Quotations Page (c) 1994–2005 QuotationsPage.com and Michael Moncur. All rights reserved. http://www.quotationspage.com/

Journal Section

MEMORIES:

LETTERS:			

e|LIVE

listen|imagine|view|experience

AUDIO BOOK DOWNLOAD INCLUDED WITH THIS BOOK!

In your hands you hold a complete digital entertainment package. Besides purchasing the paper version of this book, this book includes a free download of the audio version of this book. Simply use the code listed below when visiting our website. Once downloaded to your computer, you can listen to the book through your computer's speakers, burn it to an audio CD or save the file to your portable music device (such as Apple's popular iPod) and listen on the go!

How to get your free audio book digital download:

1. Visit www.tatepublishing.com and click on the e|LIVE logo on the home page.
2. Enter the following coupon code:
   64ae-f374-6553-0a2f-9d4f-053e-ff1f-4d4f
3. Download the audio book from your e|LIVE digital locker and begin enjoying your new digital entertainment package today!

CPSIA information can be obtained at www.ICGtesting.com
Printed in the USA
BVOW06s1408230514

354419BV00005B/35/P